7 Simple Strategies of Highly Effective Traders

T0322486

Free eBook edition

As a buyer of *7 Simple Strategies for Highly Effective Traders* you can now download the eBook edition free of charge to read on an eBook reader, smartphone or computer. Simply go to:

http://ebooks.harriman-house.com/highlyeffectivetraders

You can then register and download your free eBook.

Follow us on Twitter – @harrimanhouse – for the latest on new titles and special offers.

7 Simple Strategies
of Highly
Effective Traders

Winning technical analysis
strategies that you can put into
practice right now

Alpesh B. Patel
Paresh H. Kiri

HARRIMAN HOUSE LTD

18 College Street

Petersfield

Hampshire

GU31 4AD

GREAT BRITAIN

Tel: +44 (0)1730 233870

Email: enquiries@harriman-house.com

Website: www.harriman-house.com

@harrimanhouse

Published in Great Britain in 2014

Copyright © Harriman House Ltd

The right of Alpesh B. Patel and Paresh H. Kiri to be identified as the authors has been asserted in accordance with the Copyright, Design and Patents Act 1988.

978-0-85719-238-7

British Library Cataloguing in Publication Data

A CIP catalogue record for this book can be obtained from the British Library.

For Aekta – Alpesh's lovely wife

For Rajee – Paresh's beloved patient wife

Contents

Preface

What this book covers

We know that what traders want most is to get on with trading, so we have designed this concise book to provide quick and easy access to seven trading ideas. The seven strategies we present are straightforward, readily applicable, tried and tested, and most importantly successful.

All of the strategies presented can be applied by short to medium-term traders, such as those looking at one-minute day trading opportunities to those looking to hold positions for up to around a month, and sometimes slightly longer.

The strategies provided can be used by traders of the full range of products, from those focussed on equities to those looking at forex, bonds and commodities. Most of the strategies can also be used equally on UK, US or international markets.

With all the strategies you can trade using futures, options, CFDs or spread betting to execute the trading idea.

This book is not intended as a complete guide to trading – rather it is intended to provide the background to seven trading strategy ideas for those who are looking to develop or enhance their trading. You should make use of other trading resources, such as the internet and other books. We have provided references to useful websites where relevant throughout this book.

Who this book is for

We wrote this book for everyone from beginners to advanced traders. The beginner will get the benefit of being able to skip years of trial and error and strategy hunting, and instead be able to piggyback on our expertise and experience. We speak to thousands of traders each year through our seminars, events, webinars, blog and tweets, and know exactly the issues they face.

We've kept everything as simple as absolutely possible so that it is easy to learn and implement. Action is the key to success and the goal of this book is that you can act upon it. It is not something to just buy and forget about – it is a practical user manual. This is the next best thing to being inside a fund, looking over a fund manager's shoulder.

The advanced trader will be able to add to their existing arsenal of trading strategies or improve upon what they are already doing.

How this book is structured

We've structured this book to be compact, to the point and practical. There are seven strategies and each is broken down into an introduction, some background material, worked examples showing how to execute it and then a conclusion, which gives additional relevant information.

Most importantly, the last chapter explains three of the most important things you need to know, no matter which strategy you adopt. We've taken the best information and wisdom from our own trading, our professional experience as hedge fund managers, from our professional colleagues and from the leading hedge fund managers of the world.

Alpesh B. Patel, Hong Kong

Paresh H. Kiri, London

Acknowledgements

Our publishers of course as ever, Stephen Eckett, Myles Hunt and Craig Pearce – all of whom go together with their wonderful professional team to make the publishing experience easy from manuscript submission to printed book and book signing!

We would also like to say a big thanks to Susanne Meister at Praefinium who helped reorganise the material.

About the Authors

ALPESH B. PATEL

Alpesh is a successful entrepreneur, running an asset management company and serving as a dealmaker for the British government. Following his education at Oxford University, Alpesh became a barrister and went on to achieve remarkable success in the fields of finance, business and philanthropy, and also in his role working for the British government.

Alpesh held a weekly show on Bloomberg where he presented on technology and investing for three years. Thereafter, he set up an asset management business which survived the credit crunch and is continuing to grow internationally with offices in London, Singapore and Luxembourg.

Alpesh also had his own weekly column in the *Financial Times* for five years, for which he gained extensive praise from readers. He has previously won a *Financial Times* competition to predict the FTSE 100 over a 12-month period, beating other City professionals and asset managers – coming within 0.5% of the final value.

He is author of 18 books, which have been translated variously into Mandarin, Russian, Spanish, French, Korean, German, Thai and Polish. Alpesh's books include ones on investing online (you only need five sites and five minutes to make money); investment psychology (what the world's best self-made traders taught me that can turn you into an asset manager); outsourcing (how to do it properly to build personal capacity for game-changing achievement); and female entrepreneurs (what they do to self-sabotage and what men do to trip them up). His best selling book, *The Mind of a Trader*, was one of the top selling books on Amazon in 1999 – outselling J.K. Rowling, Bill Gates and Richard Branson for a long while.

Alpesh has sat on the advisory board of the private banking division of India's largest bank, ICICI.

PARESH KIRI

Paresh Kiri has vast experience as a floor trader on the world's second largest derivatives exchange – LIFFE – and as a portfolio manager spanning some 18 years. He is an FCA regulated investment manager.

Starting his career on the LIFFE floor in 1993, Paresh was one of the first traders to embrace screen trading, through the LIFFE online trading platform APT (Automated Pit Trading). Making progress under the guidance of legend LIFFE Trader David Kyte, he was one of the most consistent traders on the largest product on the floor – the Japanese government bond.

After successfully completing the Investment Management Certificate in 1996 he was one of the founders of Kyte Securities. So from trading financial futures and option products, Paresh had his first taste of trading stocks and shares. Over the next three years he was instrumental in designing bespoke strategies for trading equities globally.

In 2000, Kyte Securities became Eden Financial – which is now one of the most respected wealth management companies in the City of London. The strategies developed were then incorporated as the backbone of the Tomahawk hedge fund, run by Marble Bar Asset Management. That fund went on to manage over $2bn of assets.

Since leaving Eden Financial in 1999, Paresh has been managing private client and institutional money, and developing very specific operational services. He has returned to work with Kyte Group to assist in the development of an Index Options Desk. He is also seeking ways of bringing the strategies he developed to the wider public audience by structuring managed accounts services using online trading platforms.

Paresh regularly coaches and holds private seminars on trading the markets. He sits on the Advisory Board of Sterling Group, which has its HQ in Dubai (**www.sterlinggroup.info**).

Introduction

Private traders have a tendency to needlessly complicate what they do. They try strategy after strategy, sometimes using many at a time, and often not sticking with any single strategy for a prolonged period.

However, if you ask most hedge fund managers and professional traders they will tell you that trading can be kept very simple indeed. In fact, it is best kept this way. The professionals use just a few straightforward strategies and apply them time after time.

When I launched my hedge fund I had one key strategy. When Paresh co-founded his hedge fund – which went on to raise over $1 billion – it used only a handful of strategies.

The biggest difference we have identified between retail investors and professionals is that when investors are starting out they tend to chase strategies. They often try to find the ideal strategy and then move from one to another and another – wasting considerable time and money.

In this book, we will present seven simple, effective trading strategies. You can pick the ones which appeal the most to you and get on with trading and making a profit, not researching endless strategies and chasing the Holy Grail.

Different traders prefer different methods – what works for one may not appeal to another – so for the seven strategies presented here we've chosen the most effective from a variety of approaches. There is something to appeal to the momentum trader, the mean reverter, the event trader, the day trader and the longer-term investor. Basically there is something to appeal to every style. So find the strategies that resonate with you and stick to them.

The winning results of our strategies

The strategies we describe in this book work because they produce a set of results like those shown in the chart on the next page. No strategy makes money 100% of the time, but the trick is to make money on enough trades to be profitable overall.

Distribution of monthly returns in successful trading

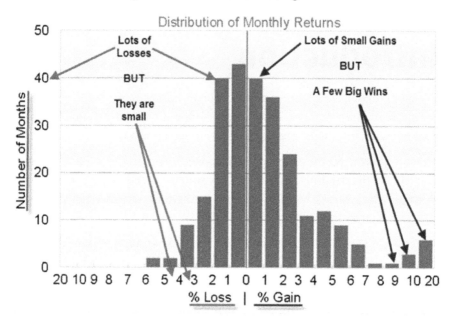

Looking at this chart in more detail, the chart below shows you where the gains and losses actually come from when applying such professional techniques. As you can see, 40% of trades return a small loss, 40% of trades return a small gain and 20% of trades produce a big win. This is a model for profitable trading.

Where the gains and losses come from in successful trading

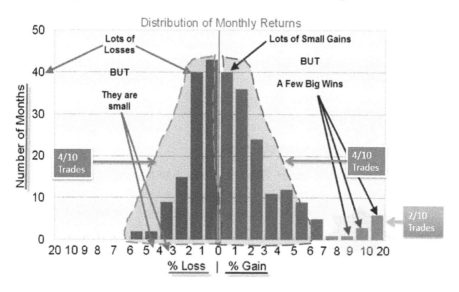

This distribution of returns grows a $1,000 investment as shown in the chart below.

The growth of a $1,000 investment

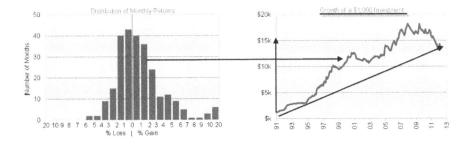

Strategy 1

Breakout With Momentum

INTRODUCTION

Our first strategy is breakout with momentum.

Breakouts occur around key support or resistance areas that have existed over multiple time frames. The most successful are the ones that occur with increased or better than average volumes. Therefore, this strategy looks to exploit situations where breakouts take place and have considerable volume behind them – it looks to trade market momentum.

Here, we use our practical experience of trading these situations to give a new slant on the traditional textbook versions of how breakouts should be traded.

All you need to put this strategy into practice for yourself is charting software which displays a clear histogram of the volume. Most charting packages nowadays have this function.

STRATEGY BASICS

The basic steps of the strategy are as follows:

1. At the point of a breakout from a trading range or a trend line, or a gap in price, we buy at the end of the breakout day (or sell if the breakout is made with momentum on the downside). This is as long as the close is within 25% of the day's high (or 25% of the day's low for a breakout to the short side).

2. This is a short-term trade and you should expect to be out of the position the very next day. However, if price continues to move in the direction of your trade then sell (or buy back for short positions) half the position and tighten stops to the previous day's high (previous day's low for short positions). You are keeping half of your position open to be able to take advantage of a new trend developing, should this happen.

3. If you have kept half of your position open let this run, with a trailing stop in place. Look for recent highs or lows as targets.

As mentioned, momentum trades are not to be considered long-term investments. Even a perfect setup – i.e. the stock closes right on its extreme and volume is there – can appear to be the correct trade the next day as the price follows through in the direction of the trade **and yet you can still lose money** if you decide that a short-term trade becomes a longer-term idea or investment. To avoid making this error, it is wise to take profits at the end of the day and keep moving your stop higher as the price moves higher.

Targets and stops

In general:

- **Day one**: If the price breaks below the previous day's low, it is likely to reverse. The whole position needs to be reassessed and possibly exited.

- **Day two**: If the price continues higher then keep the position open, as this is pure momentum. It would be pertinent to exit at least half the position if day one's low is broken. If the price continues lower and breaks the previous day's low as well it is likely the position will not continue in the direction of initial momentum and the whole position needs to be exited.

- **Day three onwards**: Exit position on any break of a previous low. However, if the price stabilises and creates a support level, exit on the lowest point of that support.

- **Targets** are harder to define as they typically revolve around support and resistance levels. Ideally, targets are set for exiting a portion of the position and a break of support levels is used for exiting the rest of the position. This lends itself to establishing short-term trading positions into longer-term investments.

Risk

We use the breakout with momentum strategy because volume-based breakouts tend to give the highest reward when compared to risk, if your short-term trade becomes a longer-term investment. The initial entry is high risk – at this stage risk-reward could be as low as 1:1 – because at this point you cannot know if this trade will follow through the next day and eventually become a long-term investment.

Risk comes in a couple of forms when considering breakout trades:

- The *overnight risk*. Breakouts tend to increase volatility so any market that moves up (or down) with increased momentum could reverse and gap down (or up) in the other direction just as quickly on the open of the next trading day. This wipes out any profits.

- The next day the stock could open unchanged, then *rally and give back much of the previous day's move as the market fills the gap*. This occurs often. As well as risk this does present an opportunity, as a spin on the breakout can be traded here, which we will discuss later in the chapter.

These momentum trades have greater risk than any other set-up as there is potential for the whole move you are trading to be erased the next day if news comes out the next morning which changes the market's view of the stock, or contradicts the direction of the move you were trading.

Stops are normally placed below the breakout, which can be relatively far away, and this adds to the risk.

A classic breakout trade setup

Figure 1.1 shows a classic breakout trade setup for 888 Holdings PLC.

Figure 1.1: breakout trade setup for 888 Holdings PLC

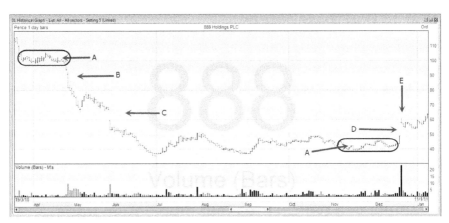

Note the following in Figure 1.1:

- **A**: The circled area marked 'A' on the left-hand side of the chart is considered to be the base. This is where the market has been ranging between two prices for a period of time. The longer the basing occurs, the greater the breakout anticipated. Here, the basing area lasted about a month. You could have traded the breakout from the base before the actual gap breakout occurred a day later (indicated by 'B').

- **B**: This is the breakout for the momentum trade to the short side. There is a gap between the close of the previous day and the opening price of the breakout move. As you can see from the volume chart below the price chart, increased volume was present with this move. The price gapped slightly lower and continued lower for the rest of the day, closing on the low.

- **C**: The same set-up as 'B' happened again at this point.

- **D**: At this point a long opportunity is presented after a basing 'A' region (the circled area on the right-hand side of the chart) that lasted for about 14 weeks.

- **E**: The long trade would have been stopped here as the follow through did not materialise. By this we mean volume did not remain high and hence momentum was not shown to be sustainable. This raises the probability that this particular gap at 'D' will be filled later.

How to find these setups

These momentum trades can be easily searched for by knowing what stocks have performed the best (for long trade opportunities) or have been the worst performers (for short opportunities) on any given day. You can find this out using Google or Yahoo Finance.

Now that we have looked at the basic aspects of the strategy, let's look at a worked example.

Example of a typical breakout momentum trade

Figure 1.2 presents a worked example of a breakout momentum trade. The stock 24/7 Real Media Inc. has broken from a base and closed on the high with more volume traded that day than usual.

Figure 1.2: breakout trade of 24/7 Real Media Inc.

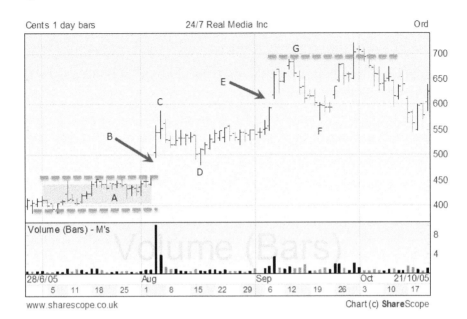

Points to note on Figure 1.2:

- **A**: The shaded area 'A' is the base area from which we expect a breakout to occur. In Figure 1.2 the price had a range of approximately $50 and the basing lasted just over a month.

- **B**: There is a price breakout from area 'A' – you can see a gap between the close of the previous day and the opening price of the breakout move. Also note that the volume exceeded recent previous levels at this point. The price is driven up and closes at $545.

The low price of the breakout day at $495 and the high price of the breakout day at $559 give us a day range of $64. To participate in momentum trades we need to see the price close not more than 25% of the daily range away from the high price (or low price for shorting breakouts).

So in this example the price must not close more than $16 from the high (range $64 x 25% = $16). It actually closed at $14 from the high (i.e. $559 – $545), and therefore within our 25% boundary.

We therefore make our entry into the trade at $545, the close of the day. We always execute such a trade on the close of the market on the breakout day (marked with 'B' in the chart) and not before.

Note that if after the breakout the price goes back into area 'A' then we would be stopped out. This would indicate a return to the resistance level of the basing area 'A' and as such the setup is invalidated. We would have placed our stop at this level when entering the trade.

Generally we have two profit exit targets for this type of trade, one for the short term and one for the long term:

1. Each time the price makes a new high we calculate for the day's range the price at a 25% drop. We then move our stop up to this level. This is of course a trailing stop.

2. We could have decided that the real stop is still the shaded area 'A', as we may have decided that this is a longer-term investment and our time horizon may be much longer than a day or two. If we think we are seeing a longer-term setup and the price develops a long-term support level then any break of this support with volume may suggest another change in trend and an immediate exit from the position.

A rule of thumb is always to sell half your remaining open trade on any weakness of the momentum. You then carry the remainder of your trade over for as long as possible. If you can keep the trade open for the longer term then you can participate in dividends and capital gain for months or years to come.

- **C**: 24/7 Real Media Inc. achieved a high of $587 the next day ('C') but closed much lower than this high.

Thinking about our first profit target mentioned above, when the price hit a high of $587 our day's range from the low of the day (at $532) is $55. Therefore our stop from the day's high is calculated as: $587 - ($55 x 25%) = $587 - $13.75 = $573.25.

If we close out now this would give us a profit of $573.25 - $545 = $28.25.

- **D**: On 17 August the price dropped into the area where the breakout (area 'B') occurred, making a low at $480. The price failed to 'fill the gap' fully and the price indeed closed up on the day, indicating underlying strength at these lower levels.

At this point we would tighten our stop at the price a few dollars below the low set on this day, say $475.

- **E**: This is another breakout and similar rules would be applied. We most likely will have been stopped out the next day as there was no follow through. So this would have been a loss for our short-term trade.

- **F**: Our longer-term investment from the position taken at E would have been stopped out at this point as the gap at point 'E' was filled the day before. What transpired is again what happened at point 'D'. The market retraced lower and closed up on the day.

We could easily re-enter the market on the close of this day – with a target at 'G', the recent high.

This is typically how we manage our breakout trades.

THE STRATEGY IN PRACTICE

We have established that trades following this strategy are short term; we are generally not looking to hold these positions for more than a week, unless the move follows through aggressively on the day after the trade is executed.

A short setup

Figure 1.3, a chart for Tate & Lyle PLC, shows how a good momentum trade can give us a trade that lasts for about four to five days. In this case the entry was short following a gap lower.

Note here that although there was a retracement higher following the short trade, the weeks that followed showed that the underlying weakness could not be averted. This is a good example of why we trim our positions by half but keep half open with the expectation that we may be able to take advantage of a longer-term trade that yields greater profit.

Figure 1.3: short trade on momentum in Tate & Lyle PLC

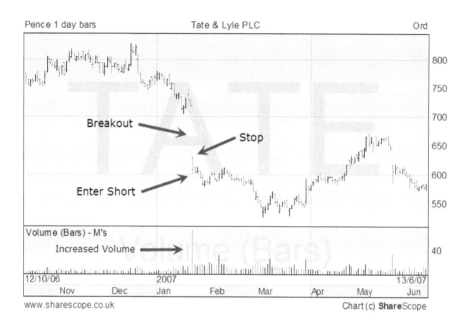

What of going long I hear you ask!

A long setup

For those who would like to see a setup for a long trade, there was an excellent opportunity in Intel Corp. on 20 April 2011 (shown in Figure 1.4).

Points to note on Figure 1.4 are as follows:

- **A**: This is the trend line from which we notice a breakout.

- **B**: The price of Intel Corp. gapped higher and closed near the high on better than average volume. This point 'B' is the day's low and the stop we apply for the next day. If momentum is to follow through to the next day then you should keep the stop as tight as possible.

- **C**: Our first profit target for exiting half our position is this resistance line 'C'. We need to be wary that Intel Corp. may not actually break through this resistance because it has reached this point twice recently and turned around.

- **D**: This is the first time the price broke through and closed below the previous day's low and it is at this level 'D' that we exit the rest of our position.

As you can see what transpired in the coming months was for the gains following the breakout to be given back and Intel Corp. made a new low in August 2011.

Figure 1.4: long momentum trade in Intel Corp.

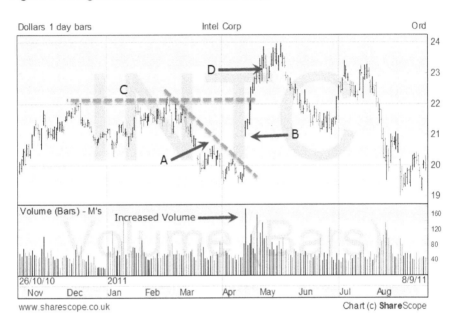

The breakout and volume combo

There is a reason why professionals look to combine a breakout with volume. Consider Figure 1.5, which shows that greater than average volume occurred in 1st Source Corp, a NASDAQ listed company, on 31 January 2012. We can describe this as a false signal.

Figure 1.5: false signal, volume only, in 1st Source Corp

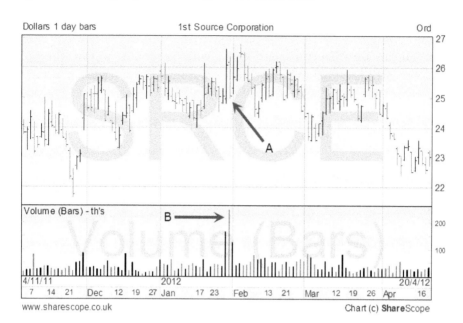

Looking at Figure 1.5:

- **A:** Price closed near the low and certainly well within 25% of the day's low, implying we would have some comfort in going short at the end of the day.

- **B:** The volume was above average, adding to the confidence in the trade to short the stock.

What we notice is the day before the potential short trade, the volume was quite high and the stock was up on the day, closing within 25% of the high for the day's total move. So we could quite easily have been long the day before.

Though this setup has volume attached it does not have a jump in price action with it and as such it is lacking the momentum we require for this strategy. This is the reason we seek to have both a breakout of some sort with the added comfort of large volume.

Potential pitfall: the blow-off move!

Beware the false breakout. The price of the breakout candle must close near the high for long opportunities or near the low for short opportunities. This is the determining factor for the trade being taken, regardless of whether the volume is there.

Refer to Figure 1.6, which is a chart for Accentia Biopharmaceuticals Inc. Although this could quite easily be a short entry the price did not close within 25% of the low on the breakout candle ('A'), as is required for a short trade.

The price rallied intraday and closed very near the high of the day at $97 on 25 March 2008 ('A'). So although the price had gapped lower, the trade opportunity was to go long at the end of the trading day. Observe that the momentum intraday seemed to suggest that there was more upside to come, most likely to fill the gap.

Figure 1.6: blow-off move in Accentia Biopharmaceuticals Inc

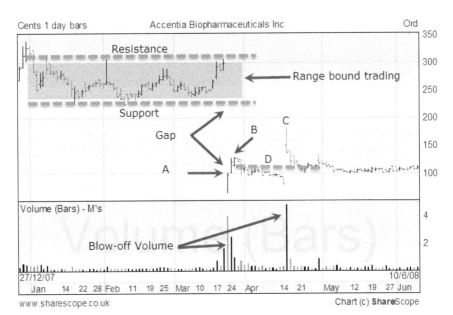

This situation is referred to as the **blow-off move**. This is when an increase in volume causes the price to move one way, but buyers (or sellers for a move in the opposite direction) take control during the day and price moves back in the other direction.

You always need to be wary of these moves and this is why we mostly execute these trades at the end of the trading day. Had we taken the short opportunity shown in Figure 1.6 on market open after the gap at 'A', thinking that this will follow through to make new lows, we would have been wrong. Always let the market tell you which trade should be taken.

As mentioned, the trade setup in Figure 1.6 is actually for a long trade. Points to note in relation to this are as follows:

- **A**: This is our entry as the market closed near the high for the day with good volume.

- **B**: This was our exit as there was no follow through of substance in the days that followed. The volume here returned to daily average the very next day and following days.

- **C**: At this point the market gapped higher and closed on the low for the day and similarly had good volume. This is another example of a blow-off trade, this time to the short side, even though the market gapped higher.

- **D**: There is a second trade setup here, this time to the short side. The target for this second trade to the short side is simply a filling of the gap, which happened five days later at 'C'.

Volatility warning

With momentum trading, expect volatility! You must have a realistic target and be ready to get out at a moment's notice if you are wrong. We illustrate this using Figure 1.7, a price chart of AGL Resources Inc.

Looking at Figure 1.7, we would have shorted the market at the gap marked in December as the volume was good and the stock closed near the low for the day. Points to note for this trade are:

- **A**: If we are trading momentum, then we are intentionally trading short-term ideas. Level 'A' is a most recent extreme low and our first profit target. We would exit half our position here, with a view to running the other half for as long as possible.

- **B**: We could have used this level as a secondary target and the other half of the trade could have been exited here. The alternative was to be stopped at a loss two days later as price at that point traded above the high of the gap day. A bounce at either levels 'A' or 'B' would have signified support at the lower levels.

- **C**: Although the market gapped lower at this point, there was no volume and so no trade was taken.

- **D**: Here we have another blow-off move. Price continued lower but rallied at the end of the day with good volume, confirming the blow-off status. Our target for going long at the end of the day here is the previous gap being filled at point 'E'.

- **E**: This is our target for going long at 'D'.

Figure 1.7: momentum increases volatility in AGL Resources Inc

Variation on momentum

Figure 1.8 shows a price chart for 1-800 Flowers.com Inc. We can see that on 24 January 2012 the price dropped 10% before rallying at the end of day to close higher. This shows that there is underlying strength in the stock.

Figure 1.8: 1-800 Flowers.com Inc

Points on Figure 1.8:

- **A**: Entry point at $272. Stop at $239.50 and with risk/reward at 1:1, we place our target at $303. We place a sell order at $303 as our exit target.

- **B**: It was not until the next day that the volume supporting our assertion that there is underlying strength in this stock appeared, as indicated in the chart at 'B'.

This is common for stocks where a certain volume above the normal market size is reported the following day (as at point B in Figure 1.8). The reason for this is to do with finessing large orders for clients and market makers.

The closing price on 26 January 2012 was $293, less than 25% from the high of the day's move, and so not a bad exit.

Example – 51job Inc

The chart of 51job Inc in Figure 1.9 provides a very good illustration of potential pitfalls with this strategy and also shows some good setups.

Figure 1.9: 51job Inc

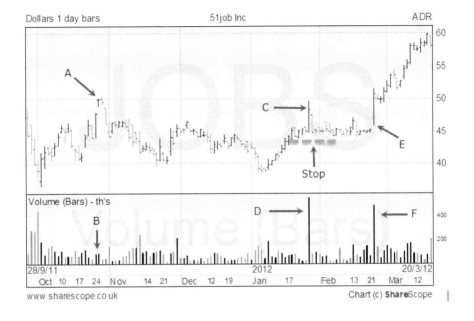

Breakout and no volume

There is an instance on this chart when we have a breakout and no volume. This does not present a momentum opportunity and so no trade would be taken.

- **A**: A breakout occurred and the stock closed very near its high.
- **B**: But we can see that volume is average.

Volume and no breakout

There is also an instance on this chart when we have high volume but no breakout. This does not present a momentum opportunity and so no trade would be taken.

- **C**: The price was up on the day and closed within the required 25% of the high. However, there was no follow through – as you can see the stock based for about a month in February 2012, with no breakout.

- **D**: There is high volume and you can see the stock made a very large single day move. We can also see a clear stop, had we bought and entered the trade. But these conditions are not enough – a breakout is needed.

Volume with breakout

Finally, there is an instance on the chart where there is a setup that combines a breakout with volume and so presents a momentum setup.

- **E**: The slight gap from the previous day's close is the breakout we need. Price closed near the high for the day. We could still use the stop we indicated previously when discussing 'D'.

- **F**: The volume is above average.

CONCLUSION

When considering these trades there are certain rules that should be regarded as gospel:

1. These are *short-term trading opportunities*. We expect in most cases to be out of the trade the very next day or within five days. However, if there is good follow through we do not wish to miss out and so we exit half the position and run the other half to seek better returns.

2. This is the only time *a short-term trade can become a long-term investment*. Most novices will get into a position that starts off well, but goes sour a day or two later. The novice will then expect the stock to return to profit and will cancel their stops in the hope that it will over time at least break even. Don't make this mistake.

3. Always put the odds in your favour: *a breakout, with a gap between the close of the previous day and the open of the next, with volume*, is the basic set of requirements.

Strategy 2

Event Trading

INTRODUCTION

Financial and economic news plays a role in moving markets, sometimes quite significantly. Studies have shown that this effect can last for up to four days as the market adjusts. Therefore, it is useful for the trader to know what market data to look out for and which markets it will move.

There is a plethora of common economic numbers that will move markets, but in this chapter we will concentrate our efforts on the most important – those that have been responsible for moving markets and creating trading opportunities for day traders.

The four data releases we will look at are:

1. Gross Domestic Product (GDP)

2. Nonfarm Payrolls (NFP)

3. Consumer Price Index (CPI)

4. Federal Open Market Committee (FOMC)

We will not be covering how to trade each of these data releases individually. You just need to let the market tell you what to do – the price action is the key determinant.

Preparation is important. Keep a close eye on the calendar of events so you know what is coming up. It will help if you have access to real-time data, available through sites such as:

- **www.tradethenews.com**
- **www.tradingeconomics.com**
- **www.ransquawk.com**

STRATEGY BASICS

For as long as there has been trading, traders have tried to anticipate the market movements after news items. This strategy does exactly that, but has the benefit that you don't have to keep watching the market. Instead you only watch it around the time of the news event itself.

The key issues are:

How do you know what news is relevant?

This comes with experience but we have highlighted four important pieces of market information in this chapter. Also many websites will tell you how important the particular announcement is and you will also get an idea from how excited CNBC get about it!

How do you know if the market will go up or down?

You can position yourself to profit through the trade by letting the market move in a particular direction first and then you either follow through or wait for the pull back. This is all explained as we go through the strategy below.

Do you place the trade before or after the news?

Many times we will place the trade after the news, but we may well place the order beforehand so that the market move gets us into the trade. This is a smart technique used by the best traders.

Why does the market fall when news is good? How am I supposed to read that? Or do I just look at the price?

We always look at the price to tell us what the market is thinking. If you are a long-term trader then you may well think the market is wrong and so buy, for instance, when prices have fallen, as you expect the market has calmed down things will return to where they were.

How do you know which currency pair for which news item?

Half the answer is always easy, for instance if the event is US GDP numbers then we know it is the USD, but against what? Oftentimes it is against any of the major currencies – GBP, EUR and JPY.

THE STRATEGY IN PRACTICE

As mentioned above, in this strategy we will look at four data releases:

1. Gross Domestic Product (GDP)

2. Nonfarm Payrolls (NFP)

3. Consumer Price Index (CPI)

4. Federal Open Market Committee (FOMC)

1. Gross Domestic Product (GDP)

GDP is considered to be the most important economic data, as it attempts to capture the state of the economy in a single number.

GDP can be thought of as all the output of an economy by individuals and corporations. It is important because it tells us whether the economy and therefore corporate profits are likely to be in good health. But as you'd expect with the markets it is not that simple. Below we go into more detail.

When and where to find this data

Many websites from Google Finance to specialist ones like InvestingBetter.com offer this kind of data. Depending on the economy this can be monthly or quarterly. It will usually impact the country's currency and its major stock indices.

So how to trade this number?

To trade the figure you have to understand that because it is an important piece of economic data – since it is about the whole of the economy – it moves the market based on pre-existing expectations. If the number exceeds expectations then the market will rise. If the number doesn't then you'd expect the market to fall. The difficult issue here is to gauge what expectations actually are because the market is made up of many participants with many expectations.

That is why the way we often trade market-moving data is to enter a trade once the market starts moving in a particular direction. The problem with this approach of course is that the market could 'fake' us, that is move in one direction, so we enter the trade, and then it moves in the opposite direction. Or it could just jump to a particular number after the announcement and so we enter the trade, and then profit taking happens so it moves against us.

Of course if we enter the trade before the figure is announced, we could simply be wrong! That is the trade-off between entering before and after an announcement. Add to this the complication that sometimes the figure will not move the market at all.

So how do traders most often trade it?

They will take a position in the currency or major stock index of the country and look to place a very short-term trade lasting minutes. Only rarely, maybe once a year, does such a figure push the market in a direction for more than a day, and by then other facts such as other data points start impacting anyway.

We for instance tend to place a trade in the direction of the market after the announcement. Of all the options open to us, this tends to work best for us and helps us make a return 7 or 8 times out of 10.

Trading example

We will look at an example from the eurozone.

On 6 March 2012 GDP data for the eurozone was released at 10:00am GMT.

The revised GDP estimate was expected to confirm that the eurozone economy contracted by 0.3% in the fourth quarter of 2011. The actual GDP came in at -0.3%, as expected.

Figure 2.1: EUR/USD on GDP data release for the eurozone

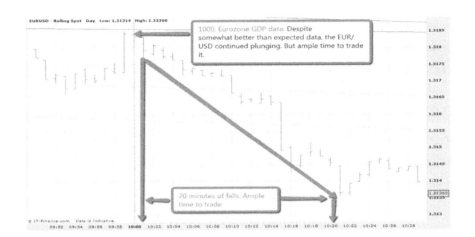

- Despite the data being just as expected, the EUR/USD continued plunging and to a low of 1.3135.

- This is tradable: notice how after 10:00am EUR/USD continued falling.

- So at this point we can establish rule 1: follow the price reaction, not your own judgement based on whether the data is better or worse than expected.

2. Nonfarm Payrolls

The US Nonfarm Payrolls (NFP) report is published by The Bureau of Labor Statistics and measures the number of jobs created in the nonfarm sector of the US economy each month.

American labour market statistics are important because they give an idea about the confidence of American businesses and consumers for the future. If jobs are being created, this leads to confidence and economic strength, and vice versa.

Thinking about how we trade this data, with nonfarm payrolls (NFP) we know that the bigger the number the more likely the USD and US equity markets will strengthen.

But by how much?

Ahead of the data release, it is useful to obtain a full range of analysts' expectations as any number that comes in at the extremes of these will definitely move the markets.

As a general rule of thumb a 10% variation either side of the expected figure will impact directly on the market in the immediate trading session. The way a day trader would be thinking is as follows:

- NFP > 10% of expectations – BUY USD

- NFP < 10% of expectations – SELL USD

- NFP = Expectation – WATCH PRICE ACTION

Whatever the outcome, we are only looking to take advantage of price volatility in the market for the first 30 minutes or so after the data release. We should be in a trade within the first five minutes.

When and where to find this data

NFP data is released on the first Friday of every month at 13:30 GMT.

You need to have an advanced broking account with real-time news feeds to access to this data, however you can get 20 minute delayed data from Yahoo Finance (**finance.yahoo.com**) or MarketWatch (**www.marketwatch.com**).

Those who wish to trade full-time will need real-time data. This can typically be sought through professional news wires like Thompson Reuters or Bloomberg. Aside from these, RANsquawk (**ransquawk.com**) offers a real-time audio service that alerts you to the economic figures as they are released and market commentary about those figures.

Trading example

We are going to take an example from 9 March 2012. The expected figure was 210,000 and the actual release was 227,000.

The actual number came in better than expected so let us now examine how and why the market reacted the way it did.

Firstly we notice that the actual number was not that far from the expected and not more than 10% above the forecast.

Figure 2.2 shows what actually happened on 9 March 2012 at 13:30 GMT when the figure was announced.

Figure 2.2: reaction of GBP/USD to NFP release

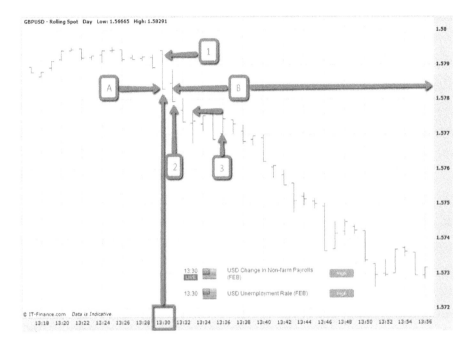

To make clear the process of how to trade this situation we will go through each minute as it occurred:

1. The NFP data is announced and comes in at 227,000. In a way, the figure itself does not matter. What matters is the price reaction. Our experience tells us this data is important – i.e. it moves the market. Alternatively, sites like **InvestingBetter.com** and **www.DailyFx.com** freely tell you what data moves the market until you have the experience to know this for yourself. These sites also tell you for which currency pairs the data will have an impact, so you know what to trade off.

2. After the first minute of trading ('1') we know our entry is one tick below the 1-minute bar's **low at 1.5783.** This is 'A' in the chart. We use this one tick below method because we want to make sure that the initial reaction, which happened to be down, will actually follow through. When it does

then we know from experience it will continue in the initial direction. We wait until the first minute has passed because that is when the big banks are often fighting it out to find a direction and we could easily be wrong-footed.

3. Notice therefore that **we are waiting for the price to get us into a trade** – not looking at whether the data beat or missed expectations.

4. As the second minute bar ('2') begins we look to enter the market on a break of the low (i.e. the price moves lower than the previous bar's low) – our entry was **1.5782**. The low on bar '1' was point 'A'. The entry for bar '2' is therefore point 'B', just below point A.

5. **Where to put our stop loss?** The stop is usually placed above the one-minute bar high. The high of bar '1' is **1.5794**. It is placed here because the principle of stop losses is that you exit a trade when you know you are wrong. Being wrong for this trade means when the price does not fall.

6. **Why the one-minute bar high?** When traders touch psychologically important levels (such as a new recent high) we are being told this is probably not just market volatility (noise) but a concerted market decision to go in one direction and not the other. Remember it is all about probabilities, not certainties. These things will probably happen, say, 7 times out of 10 – and anything more than 50-50 is an edge which can lead to profit.

7. **What about our profit target?** From our entry to our stop loss is **12 ticks**. That is our potential loss. Good trading practice dictates our profit or reward should be greater than 12 ticks, i.e. your reward-to-risk ratio is greater than 1. Actually for most traders it is 2:1. Again why? Well if you are losing only 1 for every 2 you make, then that leaves a lot of room for error and puts the odds of profit in your favour. Of course you cannot wish for a 10:1, or even a 2:1, reward-to-risk ratio. You have to look at the chart and set an appropriate target and then still exit based on market moves.

8. **So how do we know when to take a profit, given our initial target?** We look for clues that the trend is going to continue or reverse. See Table 2.1.

Table 2.1: looking for clues that the trade is going in the direction we want, or against us

Indication the trend will continue and we should add to our open positions with additional positions	Indication the trend is running out of steam and we should consider closing some or all of our open positions
The price moves below (above) the previous bar's low (high). As in bar '2' compared to bar '1'.	The price closes above (below) the previous bar's low (high) – warning, not very serious.
	The price closes above (below) the previous bar's close – moderately serious.
	The price closes above the previous bar's high – serious.
	The price closes above (below) the previous two bars' highs (lows) – very serious.
	The price does any of the above serious things for more than one bar. The more bars it continues, the more serious it is.

9. **What if you like clear-cut exit rules?** Then you could say "If the price moves above the three-period high – i.e. the highest it's been in the previous 3 bars – I will exit." We can use this method because from experience we know it is not so short a period – e.g. 1 period as to mean nothing – nor too far – e.g. 10 bars that could mean all your profits are erased. There is an example of this shown in Figure 2.2, where at bar '3' the price touches but does not exceed the three-period high. This is not a warning sign that the trend is going against us. And as you can see, after this point the price just keeps dropping in the direction of the trade for ample profits.

10. **How do you improve accuracy?** Professional traders will have more than one chart up at a time. The 1-minute chart shows the detail and all the noise that will allow them to act swiftly. A longer-term chart (5-minute) will help us remain in the trade as much of the noise will be negated.

3. Consumer Price Index (CPI)

The CPI is defined as the monthly change in prices of goods – i.e. if CPI goes up then you have inflation and if CPI goes down then you have deflation.

How we trade this is best illustrated with a trading example, as below.

When and where to find this data

Most countries release inflation data on a monthly basis. You can find this data enter 'consumer price index' and the country you are interested in into Google, e.g. 'consumer price index India', or look on sites such as **Forexnews.com**.

Trading example

This example looks at the release of German CPI data. Figure 2.3 shows an example of how **DailyFX.com** shows economic data and Figure 2.4 is the price chart at the time of the release.

Figure 2.3: website showing economic data and estimating its importance

07:00		EUR German Consumer Price Index - EU Harmonised (YoY) (FEB F)	High
07:00		EUR German Consumer Price Index (YoY) (FEB F)	High
07:00		EUR German Consumer Price Index - EU Harmonised (MoM) (FEB F)	Medium
07:00		EUR German Consumer Price Index (MoM) (FEB F)	Medium

Source: DailyFX.com

Figure 2.4: reaction of EUR/USD to the German CPI data

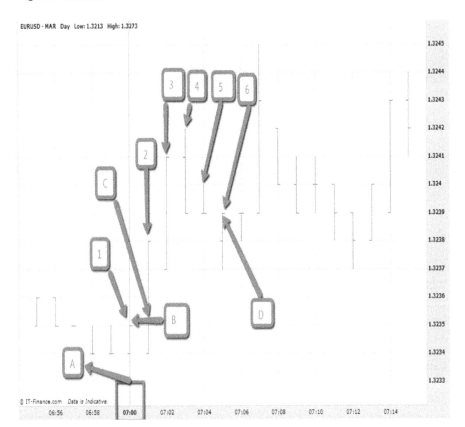

- You note from the calendar that at 07:00 (Point 'A') there is some high and medium importance economic data which will affect the euro. The chart I have chosen for the trade is EUR/USD.

- Bar '1' shows that in the first minute after the release of the news the market rose slightly to point 'B'.

- Once in the second minute after the news release (shown by bar '2') the high of bar '1' is exceeded (marked 'B' and 'C').

- We exit when the price makes a low point for two minutes because that is the lowest the price has been for the past two minutes, i.e. lower than the low points of bars '5' and '4'. This is shown by bar '6' at point 'D'.

- Our initial stop loss would have been the low of bar '1' or a two-minute low (whichever is hit first). This is because if either is breached then the momentum is not likely to continue.

- The major problem will be the bid-offer spread. During economic announcements you may get a widening of the spread, which means profit potential is reduced and the possible loss could be exacerbated. Tight spreads are essential so that your losses are limited, even in a fast-moving market.

- The alternative is to trade longer moves – but they take more time. With this trade you were done in ten minutes.

4. Federal Open Market Committee (FOMC)

The Federal Open Market Committee releases data about the US's interest rate decision. To evidence the trade setup we will look at the EUR/USD currency pair just ahead of the announcement, the reaction of the market and the trade that transpired.

When and where to find this data

This information is again found using real-time news wires. Paid-for services will give you access to the real-time news commentary that follows the announcement.

Trading example

We will look at EUR/USD for 13 March 2012. The data was due at 19:15 GMT.

A: Resistance and initial stop placed at 1.31230

B: FOMC interest rate announcement

C: Short Entry at 1.3089

D: Exit at 1.3080

Notice how we are not concerned with what the forecast and the actual data are. We only care how the market reacts and thereby moves us into a trade. How often have actual data undershot a forecast and yet the market has still risen? When traders put money into the market and create momentum – that is what we want to trade on. We don't trade on the view of some analyst who had a widely differing opinion to a hundred others – that is academic.

On the trading floor, Paresh would watch which way Goldman Sachs placed their trades, not what their analysts or CNBC said about the forecast. We are dealing with real-life trading here, not talking heads. We allow the actual price moves to move us into a trade. That is how real traders do it.

Figure 2.5: EUR/USD on 13 March 2012

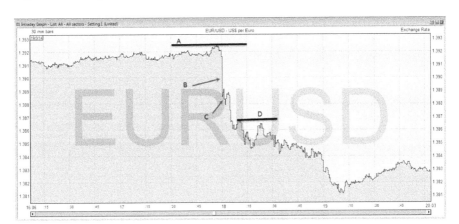

CONCLUSION

These event trading ideas follow a pattern and a set of rules that are used to help you take profits only. We do not seek to know where the market will be in three months' time, let alone the next day.

Depending on your time zone there should be an opportunity to participate in an event trading strategy every day.

The essential rules are simple enough:

- Know what economic figure is most important and most likely to move the market.

- We are not economic experts so DO NOT second-guess the direction of the move. Wait for the first minute to pass.

- Trade the break of the first minute.
- Keep stops tight.
- If you have missed the opportunity then come back another day for another event – do not chase the trade.

Strategy 3

Day Trading

INTRODUCTION

The strategy described here is the same as that used by Paresh when he was trading the Japanese Government Bond (JGB) contract on LIFFE, from 1994 to 1997. The JGB at the time was the largest contract tradable on LIFFE, where a one tick move (the smallest unit of movement in the contract) would either make or reduce your balance by approximately £140, subject to the currency level for GBP/JPY.

On the LIFFE floor, the JGB was the first contract that traded all day on what was known as the APT – Automated Pit Trading. All other futures contracts would trade in typical pit conditions, forming the colourful ensemble that was showcased in movies like *Trading Places*.

Paresh was working with guidance from legendary trader David Kyte. On his first day he traded two lots and, with trading opening at 07:00, by 07:15 he was down £8,600.

David could have asked Paresh to do any number of things, such as to leave the firm and not come back, but instead he suggested that going back down on the floor and trading the loss back was the best thing to do.

The methodology described below is the one Paresh used to make this one-day loss back and be in profit at the end of 12 months, trading solely one product, one idea and one lot. The idea was spawned from the wisdom of David Kyte after Paresh's first and worst ever day trading on LIFFE.

David's advice was:

1. Risk daily £1,000.

2. If you lose £1,000 stop trading for the day.

3. If you lose £1,000 two days in a row then you will help the trainee runners. (Runners were the lowest position on the floor.)

He advised Paresh to develop a trading style through taking small losses. He said, "Always arrive before the market opens. Know what has moved the market in Japan. And one other thing – be sure never to leave before the market closes."

Developing a disciplined trading approach

This advice formed the bedrock of the discipline that followed. David Kyte was not telling Paresh how to trade or pick trading opportunities, he was saying simply "Do not lose." Fight for the right to stay in the game by sticking to your trading plan – and the bones of that trading plan is how you **manage your risk**. The rest will follow.

The three simple points above focussed his mind and formed the building blocks of the right trading habit. They taught the importance of being completely detached from the outcome of any particular trading day.

There were no computer screens with complicated charting packages. Just a simple Reuters terminal was present on each desk to display economic data and generic financial market news. The only information available at the end of the trading day in Japan, at 6:00am GMT, was the daily range on that day, i.e. the JGB's open, high, low and close.

With limited information and no charting package traders were left to their own instincts to create strategies that would help generate a profitable outcome for the day. Each trader created his or her special strategy, which comprised of:

1. How much to lose on any given day.

2. What will the trader do if the stop loss target for the day is reached?

3. Does there have to be a target for how much the trader wishes to make on any given day?

The strategy developed from asking these three questions. Let's now look at the thought process behind this strategy in a bit more detail by answering these questions.

STRATEGY BASICS

1. How much to lose on any given day

David Kyte was clear – he gave a daily £1,000 stop loss. Considering it took 15 minutes to lose more than £8,000, this seemed to be quite a task. So far all Paresh knew was how to lose £8,600 in quarter of an hour. David did say, "If you can lose £8,600, then you know that you can make that in a day!"

So the first rule Paresh made was to set a maximum **£500** stop loss for the day. This is fine as a rule, but it also limited the size that he could trade. For Paresh to ensure a loss greater than this did not occur – given a single one tick movement was going to put at risk about £140 – he could only trade **1 lot**. This meant the stop for a trade was always about 3 to 4 ticks away from entry, i.e. 4 x 140 = £560. This forces one to pick the levels with precision, as a 4-tick movement is not a lot and the spread alone was at the best of times 2 ticks.

But, this is not enough. What if Paresh did lose two days in row, with a self-inflicted allowable risk of £500? There had to be a forfeit. This was simple enough. Leaving the trading screen was not an option so Paresh decided on a forfeit that entailed watching the market the next day all day if a loss the previous day transpired.

2. What will the trader do if stop loss target for the day is reached?

No matter how much he wanted to pull the trigger, if a loss occurred the day before then Paresh would just watch the market on the second day. This prevented him from having two losing days in a row. He still arrived at 06:00 GMT and still analysed the previous night's range for Japan, but would sit on his hands the whole day and not trade. This helped to develop that gut instinct to ensure if he pulled the trigger he was 90% certain that the trade was going to be a winning one.

The APT had a unique aspect which included:

1. You could see who was on the bid or the offer, and

2. You could see the depth of the market, i.e. you could see all the orders on the buy side and the sell side below and above the best bid and offer.

This helped with confidence – if one could see there was support or resistance at a particular price by knowing who was providing the liquidity (i.e. the volume), one could join the price or be the market, which means tightening the spread and being the actual market maker.

Also if you know which bank or organisation was on the bid and offer then this would add to confidence that the support or resistance is very real. Banks would not spoof the market, which many local traders on LIFFE often did to rout out the real orders from clients of the banks.

3. Does there have to be a target of how much to make for the day?

The simple answer is **no**!

The focus should be solely on prevention of losing and getting into a trade knowing that you will only lose £500, but if the market begins to move in the anticipated direction then we must move the stop accordingly. This was achieved by having a mental trailing stop that would allow the market to breathe. To have a target price would have made sense only if you had access to potential support and resistance lines.

There was however one place you could put a target price in – but this was more relevant when trading more than two lots at a time. The target would be used to get out of half the position by selling one lot and then letting the second lot run. This again created discipline in ensuring that profits were always banked. At the same time it meant that another entry point did not have to be sought if we wanted to get back into a position – often it would be the case that when trading a one lot position it was hard to get into a new position again once you have traded out of it.

The strategy can be used in any market

Finally, this trading idea works in any market, as will be discussed below, but it is especially good in fixed income and indices. This will be our main focus.

It is important to note that the Japanese Government Bond market in the UK time zone was VERY illiquid and so we cannot use precisely the same terms of trading. Each market will have its own nuances and behaviour that will impact on how we best approach the hourly breakout strategy. We shall now go through daily market behaviour using one-minute charts to gauge how best to day trade the more liquid fixed income and index markets.

THE STRATEGY IN PRACTICE

Trading with one lot

The first two hours of trading

The markets open at either 7:00am or 8:00am, depending on market and location. You need to decide which market you wish to trade and be ready in time for the open. The UK Gilt market opens at 08:00 GMT.

Figure 3.1 shows the UK Daily Gilt Future on 25 June 2014. There is a range of 26 ticks – i.e. 109.415 to 109.675 – in the first hour of trading. The market has shown us two points that we will now use for our initial entry signal.

The strategy is simple enough:

- **Buy** – go long – on the break of the high 109.675 after the first hour of trading.

- **Sell** – go short – at the break of the low 109.415 after the first hour of trading.

Figure 3.1: UK Daily Gilt Future, 25 June 2014

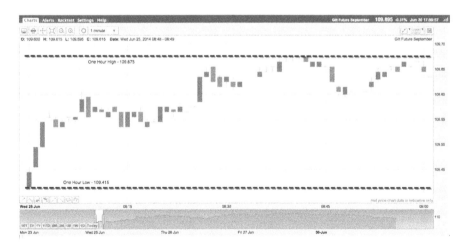

The basic rules:

- On any break look to make 3 to 5 ticks, as we are not looking to find a long-term move, just an opportunity to bank some profits.

- Once profits are banked, we have put odds in our favour that we are less likely to lose for the day. If all you do is bank, say, 3 ticks a day this way then for the Gilt Future – where the tick value is £10.00 – you are banking £30 a day, or £150 pounds a week. You can see how just by being selfish and not overly clever in trying to suggest a target we have a tool to help us with basic cash flow.

- NB – This is the only strategy where the risk is greater than the perceived reward. But we are usually in and out of the trade within ten minutes, as can be seen in Figure 3.2.

Figure 3.2: Daily Gilt Future, 25 June 2014, the next hour

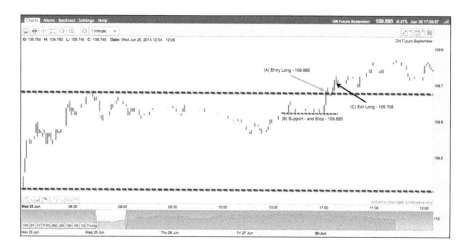

- **A**: Entry point 109.685 – 1 tick above the hourly high.

- **B**: This point is the most logical support and is actually 6.5 ticks lower – 109.620, so our stop is a tick below this point. The risk is therefore 7.5 ticks.

- **C**: Our target is about 3 ticks for the first trade and we achieved this at 109.705 (note that this was not the high for the period).

The full trading day

So let us now look at the whole trading day from 08:00 to 17:00 on 23 June 2014 and go through how many opportunities there are in a single day. Our aim is to make at least one trade a day, so if more do not appear then that is fine. The goal is to be positive at the end of the day without having an overnight position and hence overnight risk.

Figure 3.3 shows the chart on 23 June and indicates the trading opportunities.

Figure 3.3: Daily Gilt Future, 23 June 2014, full trading day

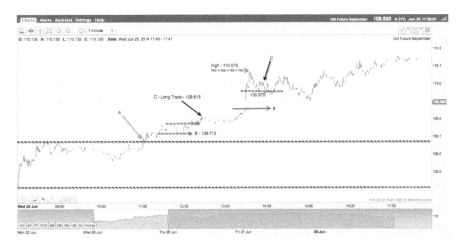

- **A:** This was our opening trade, the breakout of an hourly range. We look to always make a small profit on these and look to build on the profit through the course of the trading day. These days technology allows us to assess possible support and resistance lines, as drawn in Figure 3.3, to help us negotiate appropriate entry and exit levels.

- **B:** Having picked a break of the high the natural assumption would be to seek to go long. At this level we notice some support at 109.715. This point could be a good level to have a stop, if we make a new high above 'A'.

- **C:** We took a second long trade at this point as it was above the previous exit we had with trade 'A'. The stop, as mentioned, is below 'B'. Again we are seeking to make about 3 ticks and we exited 75 minutes later at 109.970. With an entry at 109.815 we made a little more than expected, i.e. 16.5 ticks. Our tally for the day is 19.5 ticks profit.

- **D**: Around here if we were to allow our gut to react and say "Hey 110.075 may actually be the high for the day," then we could attempt to go short. We did not – but you could suggest 109.970 is not a good support and may actually be a better resistance line.

- **E**: If we did go short then our exit would be along this line, as normally what transpires is that the market will test the lower levels before moving higher, or in this case try and fill the gap. What actually happened is that 110.075 was not the high for the day and the market continued higher, but in a sideways motion, making any other opportunity to either go long or short difficult to assess.

Summary

1. We start the day with a single, positive focus.

2. Do not risk more than you have made on the first trade if you can avoid it.

3. Never lose more than your stated daily maximum loss.

4. Do not be afraid to pull the trigger and be wrong.

Alternative to trading just with one lot

Once we have developed a feel for the market and banked some real profits we need to begin increasing the size we trade. As we do this, we need to pick our levels more deliberately as more is at stake. We will demonstrate this using a five-minute chart and using our basic break of an hourly range as our reason to enter a trade.

The German Bund opens at 07:00 GMT. Figure 3.4 shows the Bund for 19 March 2012. This clearly shows why we cannot just trade the breakout of an hourly range. The first break long came back within the hourly range indicated between 135.94 and the low 135.58.

Figure 3.4: German Bund Futures, one-day chart, 19 March 2012

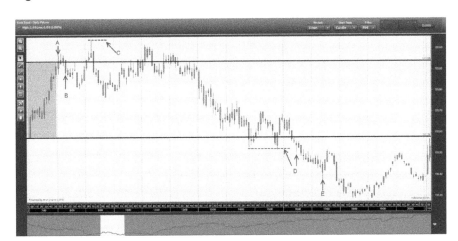

- **A**: First entry on break of hourly high at 135.98.

- **B**: Stopped out at 135.88 – our tally for the day on 19 March 2012 is negative 10 ticks.

- **C**: Although we were stopped out a new high was set. Figure 3.5 – a two-day futures chart – explains graphically why we did not seek to go long at this point. As we extrapolate 'C' to the left we notice that on Friday 16 March, the previous trading day, there is a potential resistance line at this level (shown in Figure 3.5).

- **D**: Referring to Figure 3.4 again, we went short at 'D', where the price was 135.50.

- **E**: At the exit at 'E' we looked only to make back our loss from the previous trade earlier in the day. The low was 135.38. Having put a limit to only make back the loss we were out at 135.40, even though the price did touch 135.29.

Figure 3.5: two-day Bund Futures Chart, 16 March and 19 March 2012

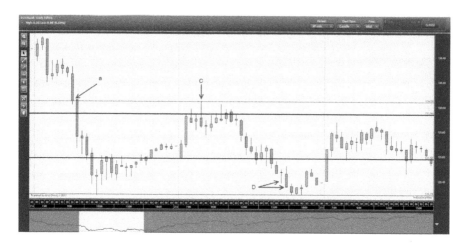

Using support and resistance to pick your trades for the rest of the day

Figure 3.6 shows a five-day chart of the daily Bund Future. We make the following assessment: 135.29 is a strong support now as the price has bounced from this point three times. Using a 30-minute chart we notice doji patterns. A doji pattern is a Japanese candlestick where the price has opened and closed at the same price in that time period. It signifies a possible change in direction.

We trade using a breakout on the hourly chart as the core entry.

- **A**: The shaded area 'A' shows the tight one-hourly range and we enter a long position at 135.52, with 4 lots. Our stop is 135.27 as we are looking at a potential larger move. With 4 lots and risking 10 euro per tick, we are risking 4 x (135.52 - 135.27) x 10 = 4 lots x 25 ticks x 10 euro = 1,000 euro.

- **B**: Our first resistance line where we exit half the position.

- **C**: Exit the rest of our position. We ensure we do not carry overnight positions.

We would certainly need to have patience for such an 'A grade' setup to transpire. Notice how we used more than the simple breakout – we looked into the past to see where the price of the market has been before and sought to develop expected support and resistance lines that would determine our appropriate stops and limit targets.

Figure 3.6: German Bund Future, five-day chart

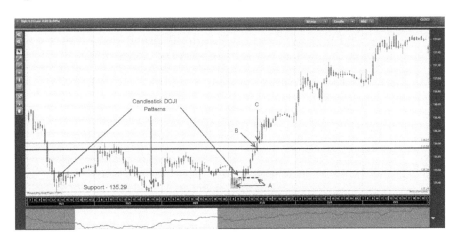

Hourly breakout trade for the S&P 500 Index

Figure 3.7 shows the S&P 500 on 5 April 2012. The range for the first hour was 1389.90 to 1394.60. The tick value is $12.50 for each quarter point move, i.e. a full point is equal to $50.

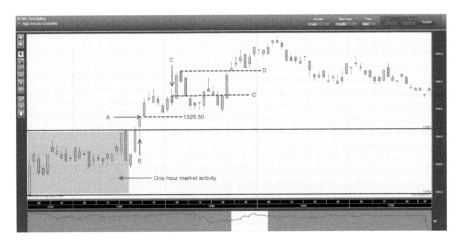

- **A:** Our first entry at which we bought two lots at 1395.50. The shaded area is the first hour's activity, which begins at 13:30 GMT when the US markets open. This point becomes our stop as the market moves ahead in time.

- **B**: Our stop could be just below the breakout line at 1394.60, or below the bar where the breakout occurred as indicated by 'B' at 1394.

- **C**: Our first lot was exited at 1397.00 with the second lot allowed to stay open to make the most of any further potential upside move.

- **D**: We exit our second lot at this point – 1398.80 – at 15:40 GMT as the market attempted to break through this high set half an hour prior.

No more opportunities presented themselves after this.

The overall point once again is that we are looking to just bank the cash. This will help build confidence and understanding of market activity.

CONCLUSION

This strategy is really good for beginners who do not wish to be inundated with indicators and complexities that may require a statistics degree to understand. Also no complicated charting package is required, just the detail of the most recent high and low for the day.

The concept is simple. After the first hour you can be sure that any overnight rounding of positions by professional traders at large institutions will have finished. The rest of the day is all about the battle between buyers and sellers, demand and supply.

The skill is having discipline. This instils the correct money management for this trade setup. Do not risk more than **2%** of your overall capital on **any single day**. If your account is opened with £10,000 then look to lose £**200 only** per day. This means you should be looking to make £**200 or more for the day also**. Do not risk more than the profit you have made in a day if you are up. Be aware that trades of this type typically do not fall into the category of having the perfect **risk-to-reward ratio**.

As you begin trading the markets, start small. Paresh started off with a one lot and using only the one lot breakout of an hourly range was in profit by the end of his first 12 months by about £25K. This was after making his first day loss of £8,600 back.

Strategy 4

Mean Reversion

INTRODUCTION

The essence of our fourth trading strategy is that prices have a tendency to go back to where they have been in the recent past. The principle is known as mean-reverting – it implies that 90% of the time the price will not move in any trend but just back and forth around a set point for a period of time.

This strategy is used by professionals and novices alike so it should be simple enough for any trader to apply.

STRATEGY BASICS

The principle of mean reversion

Figure 4.1 depicts the essential concept of mean reversion, which is that there is an area of value around which a price will oscillate. We can see that 70% of trades take place in the area around the mean price. Knowing this allows us to take advantage of the fact in our trading.

Figure 4.1: the principle of mean reversion

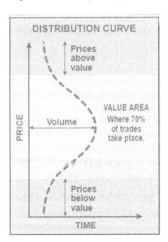

Strategy rules

The essential rules of the strategy are as follows:

Entry

- Draw by estimate a mean reversion line.

- Go long as price falls (or vice versa).

- Start with a small $1 per point profit or loss. For example, if GBP/USD rate moves 0.0001 you should make $1. Build trade size so that any exit at a loss is 2% of your total trading capital.

Exit

- If price hits the mean reversion line or your stop loss.

We will elaborate more on these rules as we work through the examples below.

Drawing the mean reversion line on the chart

Let's take a look at Figure 4.2, showing GBP/USD. This is a three-minute chart, so each individual bar represents three minutes of price moves. (We could quite easily have chosen a five minute or a 30 minute chart.) These charts are available from all the main providers of online platforms like Capital Spreads or ETX, who provide charting free as part of their brokerage services.

Drawn on the chart is a horizontal line at the price of 1.551, which is the best guestimate of the average or mean around which the price is moving. Price is seemingly reverting to this mean and if it gets too far away from it we would expect it to move back towards it again.

Some software will draw this line for you under what's called a 'linear regression' – this is a statistician's way of saying the average price over a period of time, or line of best fit. In a fast trading environment we can draw our own linear regression line, saving time to get on with the activity of trading.

For each different time frame the mean would of course be different and thereby so would our trades. An example is also shown below for daily charts (see Figure 4.3).

Figure 4.2: GBP/USD three-minute chart

So who uses the three-minute chart?

Someone who is trading actively during the day. They may even trade on the one-minute chart. They do this because it gives them lots of trading setups and allows them to deploy their capital and earn a return on this capital.

Figure 4.3 is a daily chart for GBP/USD, where each bar represents the high, low, open and close for the day (i.e. the day's range). The average or mean comes in at around 1.58. Again the idea is that if the price extends too far away from this, either above or below, then we can expect the market to tend to come back towards 1.58.

Figure 4.3: GBP/USD daily chart

The question you will be asking is, does the price revert to the mean often enough to profit from it?

In short, yes. But given that if it didn't we could be stuck in a trade waiting for it to come back to its mean price we must put in stop losses to protect our capital.

This strategy developed because predicting trends intraday is not the best use of time. Traders want to have a better idea of where the price is heading based on where it has been, not where it might go based on where it has never been. This enables them to be actively trading, making the most of short-term intraday opportunities that emerge.

Two more examples

Below are two more illustrations. Figure 4.4 is another example of a daily reversion mean opportunity in EUR/USD. It shows 1.37 as an area around which the price seems to be mean reverting.

Figure 4.4: GBP/USD daily chart showing 1.37 as a mean reversion area

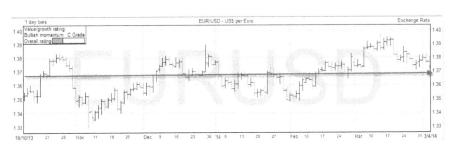

Figure 4.5 shows an example where GBP/USD does not revert to the mean over the period February 2014 to May 2014. If we had expected the price to return to the region of 1.64 we would have waited a long time and potentially suffered a large loss.

Figure 4.5: GBP/USD showing no mean reversion on the daily chart from February 2014 to May 2014

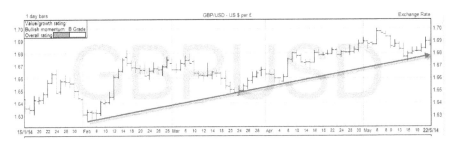

Every now and then the market will move away from the most recent range that forms the basis of this strategy. As long as we have our stops in place then we will be out of the trade and ready to participate the next time the market begins its mean reversion.

THE STRATEGY IN PRACTICE

Mean reversions are excellent for day trading and certainly most charting packages will have some kind of oscillator for you to define the most likely mean reversion point in any given time frame. We shall explain the methodology using Figure 4.6, a three-minute chart for GBP/USD.

Here the mean reversion line is at 1.5525. Our entry is at point 'A' at 1.5500. Point B is the worst price reached while we are in the trade and point 'C' is where we get out, at 1.5525. We will explore this trade in more detail below.

Figure 4.6: GBP/USD three-minute chart

Planning your trade according to your psychology

1. **Choose your time frame.** If you intend to be a day trader, sitting in front of the computer, then a three-minute or five-minute chart would be more

than adequate. If instead you are trading part-time, then a daily chart may be better, where each bar is the range for the whole day.

2. **Choose a mean reversion line.** We need sufficient data points upon which to form a mean around which price oscillates. Only then can we choose a mean reversion line. In Figure 4.6 we have marked where we believe the mean is using a horizontal line. Over 100 historical bars are covered by this line. This clearly shows that for quite a while the price has been moving around this mean of 1.5525 and the assumption can be made that the price will continue to do so. This can be estimated by eye when you look at the chart, which is how most day traders will do it. Most trading platforms with charting facilities will allow you to add a linear regression line between a historic point and today's price.

3. **Choose an entry point.** At which price do we trigger a trade? Going back to Figure 4.6, let us consider point 'A' that represents a point where price had moved too far from this mean and will revert back to it. We could have picked this point using complicated statistical measures such as standard deviations, but let's keep it simple. Our entry is 1.5500 because:

   - It looks like a level which the price tends not to reach frequently.

   - It's far from the mean and so likely to result in a good opportunity to make a profit.

   - It's not so far from the mean that it is the start of a whole new trend.

   - If the price is at a round number then most likely we will see some support or resistance around this point intraday.

So, to recap, the entry is 1.5500 and the mean reversion line is at 1.5525. We are looking to exit when price gets back to the mean reversion line at around point 'C'.

Profit targets and stop losses

So how much can I make from this trade?

Well, if I made $1 for every point from entry to exit at the mean reversion line, then I would make $25 (1.5525 - 1.5500). Of course you can trade multiples of that, depending on how much trading capital you have, but more on that in a moment.

Prices will never move in a straight line and it may take time to get to our target. Given that the price in one trade can take several hours to reach our target, we should be prepared to trade on multiple currencies and commodities, having placed multiple positions in varying time frames.

This diversifies risk, assuming they are not all the same time frame of three minutes and all USD trades. Even then, you would want to be non-correlated, i.e. your trades should not all be moving in tandem, which will prevent you from exposing your capital to a singular large risk.

Point 'B' represented our worst moment in this trade when the price went as low as 1.5485. At that point we were sitting on a paper loss of 1.5500 - 1.5485 = $15.

How did we know not to exit at that point? Or put another way, what is our stop loss, the point at which we exit with a loss? We cannot hold on forever taking an endless loss all in the hope of making $25.

If the stop loss is equal to the profit to be achieved, i.e. $25, then that is a good measure.

You may have spotted that if we win $25 when we win and lose $25 when we lose, we don't make any money. This is true – in fact, after brokerage costs, we would be losing a little. However, this is where the principle of mean reversion comes in. If we expect prices that have fallen quite far to rebound to the mean as if on a bungee rope, then we expect to win more often (i.e. prices extended from the mean revert back to it) than lose (i.e. prices go on extending and make ever greater losses and do not mean revert).

So imagine we were therefore expecting to be right – the price reverts back to mean – six times out of ten, and wrong four times out of ten.

Then our results would look like this:

- Profits = 6 x $25 = $150
- Losses = 4 x $25 = $100
- Overall profit per ten trades = $50.

The risk of placing larger trades

It looks like we have just found a profit-making machine. If so, why would we just not make bigger bets, such as ten times the size? The answer is, what if we have a string of losses? Imagine we placed trades 100 times larger and we had five losing trades in a row. We would be down 5 x $2,500, that is

$12,500. If your total trading capital was $12,500 then you would be wiped out.

Okay, but suppose your trading capital is not merely $12,500. How do you then decide how much to bet in each trade to maximise your return? After all you don't want to make a pathetic $25 now that you've discovered a profit-making strategy.

As mentioned, you should lose no more than 2% of your trading capital when you are wrong. If you have $12,500 then that means you should lose no more than $250 when you are wrong on any one trade.

Using the same pattern of wins and losses for every ten trades as in the example above, that would mean you would have six $250 winning trades, making you $1,500, and four $250 losing trades, losing you $1000. Overall for every ten trades you would make $500 profit.

Further thoughts on mean reversion

The key to executing this strategy successfully is in how well you exercise discipline. Stick to your trading plan and do not get too greedy or too confident.

You may consider entering the trade at closer to the mean reversion line as, after all, the price will revert. It is true you could do this, setting your stop loss proportionately. But you will potentially make less money, because the move back to the mean is small from a closer entry point.

Okay, you ask, why then not increase the bet size and trade from a closer distance?

There is nothing wrong with that, as long as you stick to your stop loss. The problem is that the price could just keep hitting your stop loss, i.e. continuing to move away from the mean reversion line. The point of us picking point 'A' in the example above was that the price was unlikely to go beyond that based on recent price action.

Imagine an elastic band – the more you stretch it, the faster and more power it possesses to revert to a balanced state. Trade too early and you risk being stopped out too often; trade too late and you may be on the wrong side of a new trade and a new mean being sought by the market.

Another thing you may consider is entering closer to the mean reversion line and putting your stop loss a lot further out. The answer is that you could do this as long as [number of winning trades] x [$profit per winning trade] is greater than [number of losing trades] x [$loss per losing trade].

So imagine you entered if the price moved $10 away from the mean reversion line and your stop loss was $100 away. That is if you suffered a $100 loss you would exit. This is fine as long as you had ten winning trades for every losing one.

Let us have a look at Figure 4.7, which is another GBP/USD daily chart. You place a stop loss very far away. You then just keep entering trades as you see fit as soon as they move from the mean reversion line. *What could go wrong?*

Well, as mentioned, you could have a string of losses and wipe out your account. This could happen if you opened all the positions indicated in Figure 4.7 with the label 'Entry Points' and your stop loss was hit each time.

We avoid that by following the rules of limiting our bet size and making sure that if we have a string of, say, five consecutive losing trades then we do not come even close to wiping ourselves out. In fact, five consecutive losing trades should lose no more than a total of 10% of our total trading capital.

Figure 4.7: GBP/USD daily price chart

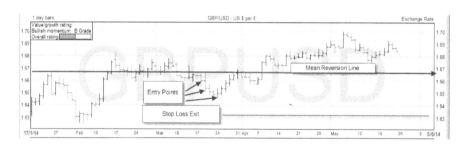

CONCLUSION

Presented below are actual trading results from applying this strategy. Figure 4.8 shows 454 trades placed in the first two weeks of July 2008. 450 trades won.

Each horizontal line shows the level of profit per trade. The profit is not exactly equal for each trade because this represents all trades, across all time frames and all products, using this strategy.

Figure 4.8: results from trading the mean reversion strategy

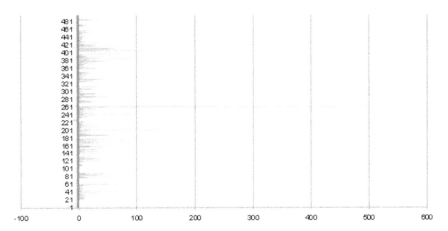

Strategy 5

Moving Averages

INTRODUCTION

Moving averages come in various forms but their underlying purpose remains the same: they show the ebb and flow of the market as it evolves over time and help technical traders track the trends of financial assets by smoothing out the day-to-day price fluctuations, or noise. Moving averages are called lagging indicators as they are calculated from past prices. They are used as the basis for many other technical indicators, such as Bollinger Bands and MACD.

Moving averages do not predict the future price direction on their own; however, this strategy will help you to use them to predict a probable change in direction.

STRATEGY BASICS

Moving averages come in several guises but we will only consider two varieties for use in this strategy:

1. **Simple moving average** – used to smooth out short-term fluctuations and highlight potential trends that are taking place. It is an unweighted average of the previous n price points – which usually is the close price for the period. The period can be made of any time frame we desire, whether monthly, daily, hourly or five minutes.

2. **Exponential moving average** – similar to the SMA, except these are weighted – with greater weighting given to the more recent prices in the time period, at the same time reducing the weighting of the older time period. This makes the EMA a lot more responsive to recent price movements.

For your reference the other moving averages include:

• Adaptive Moving Average
• Triangular Moving Average

- Typical Price Moving Average (Pivot Point)
- Weighted Moving Average (WMA)

Charting software which allows you to add both a **simple moving average (SMA)** and an **exponential moving average (EMA)** is pretty much all you need.

Moving averages work in all time frames and generally are most popular with foreign exchange and stock indices traders, i.e. those trading the most liquid markets.

The typical approach to trading with SMA and EMA is to look for a crossover; this is when two moving averages of different durations cross. A crossover alerts the trader to a potential change in trend, whether up or down. Many large investment banks will look to the SMA, or SMA and EMA crossover setups, to make longer-term trading assumptions.

The most popular use of moving averages by professionals will be explored through the rest of this chapter, with examples that highlight the pitfalls and the success stories.

50-day and 200-day simple moving average (SMA)

Two of the most popular moving averages that trading institutions look at are the 50-day and 200-day. They are used to evaluate longer-term trends that are set to continue or about to change. They also offer good support and resistance areas for markets over time.

Example: FTSE 100

The following chart shows the FTSE 100 Index for 2002-2014 with the 50-day and 200-day moving averages added.

Figure 5.1: FTSE 100 Index with the 50-day and 200-day simple moving average

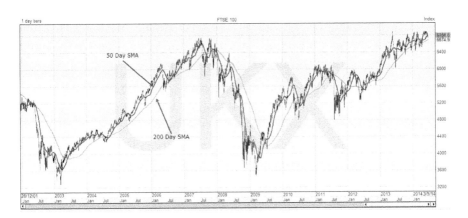

Notes:

- You will notice how well the 50-day SMA hugs the price, while the 200-day plays catch up.

- From around March 2003 we witness the low of the market set in but the 50-day and the 200-day SMA crossed over much later – indicating a change in trend of the moving averages – in June 2003. From this alone we can see that the lag for a daily chart is about four months. In June 2003 we could have taken a long position at this crossover.

- The 50-day SMA is used to alert us to weakness and we should be tightening our stops or watching closely as the market gets close to the 200-day SMA. To set stops, a lot of traders use ATR – average true range. ATR refers to the average price range of the trading in the period we are looking at. In this case the daily price range for four months would be appropriate because it is a quarterly review of events and will define what the average ATR and price range may be for the following quarter. This average is our ATR called N. Our stop would then be placed at 2N (i.e. twice the average price movement for the period).

- In the period 2003 to 2007 the price dipped below the 200-day SMA twice in the move up – but it never breached our 2N rule, which kept us in the trade from June 2003 through to July 2007.

Moving averages work best in pairs. The example above is a typical professional setup where both the 200-day SMA and 50-day SMA are displayed. When they cross it indicates a high possibility of a change in trend. Normally the shorter time frame – in this case the 50-day – acts as the **signal line** and dictates where the market may be heading.

To time the trade, this crossover of moving averages works best where a new high or a new low is being set. You need to look for prolonged uptrends or downtrends that will eventually fail at new highs or new lows – if you can find these areas you stand the chance of participating for the bulk of a new directional move for the market.

In the ten years between 2002 and 2012 it has been observed that a change in direction in the FTSE 100 occurred pretty much every four years. Of course this pattern may not hold true into the future.

Looking for additional evidence

To make your assessment more secure you need to look for additional evidence. We show this in Figure 5.2, which is a chart of the FTSE 100 with an SMA crossover of price after a double top has been set.

Figure 5.2: SMA crossover in FTSE 100

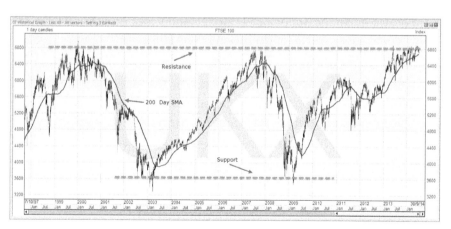

Double tops are formed when the market has attempted to test a previous high and fails, turning around just above, just below or at the same price as the previous high.

Looking at the chart, we can see the all-time high in the FTSE 100 in 1999, a new low in 2003, then the market advanced to another high in 2007, establishing a double top and a change in direction that saw the market test the low of 2003 in 2009 – creating a longer-term double bottom.

If you know the general direction of the trend then as long as the market stays above the longer-term SMA (200-day SMA in this example) we should be looking to go **long when price is above the line and short when price is below the line**. As mentioned, the 50-day SMA is the signal line and hugs the price. You can see that it does this in Figure 5.2, where it is barely distinguishable from the price movement.

The skill is in knowing where to place your stop. This is normally sought at the point where we know we have been proved wrong, i.e. in this case when the market moves aggressively through both lines. You must **allow for market noise** – as you can see in 2006 we could have been stopped out twice had we not set an exit at a point **2 x ATR away from the 200-day SMA**. The 2N stop could be quite expensive for long-term trading, but as you can see the profits can be substantial.

Now we will move on to discuss the shorter-term signals.

Shorter-term moving average signals

Professional trading companies use a combination of SMAs and exponential moving averages (EMAs). A typical combination is the 24 SMA and the 10 EMA.

The EMA acts as an indicator that will hug the price and is the signal line. The SMA is used as a place to be stopped should the market trade through it. This is illustrated in Figure 5.3 with the AUD/USD forex pair.

The EMA **weighs current prices more heavily than past prices**. This gives the **EMA** the advantage of being quicker to respond to price fluctuations than a simple moving average; however, that can also be viewed as a disadvantage because the EMA is more prone to whipsaws (i.e. false signals).

Figure 5.3: AUD/USD with EMA/SMA crossovers

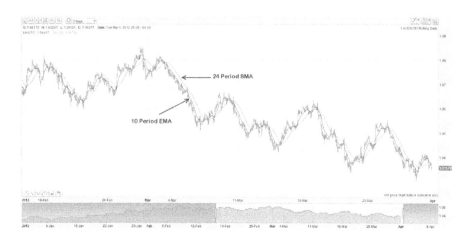

Points to note:

- The 10-day EMA hugs the price and the 24-day SMA lags the price.

- Stops are usually placed at 2 x ATR from the SMA line, so you are not whipsawed out of positions.

- This does not work at all well in sideways markets, e.g. between 19 February 2012 and 27 February 2012.

Moving averages should be used as part of an arsenal of tools that aid confirmation of the direction of the market, whether **sideways, up or down**.

STRATEGY IN PRACTICE

50 and 200 SMA for stocks

To show the importance of the moving average crossover we will look at Lehman Brothers Holdings Inc, shown in Figure 5.4.

Professionals will target a strategy depending on where the market stands with respect to the 200-day moving average. If the price is above the 200-day SMA then strategies that employ going long will be sought and conversely if the market is below the 200-day SMA, short opportunities will be sought.

Figure 5.4: Lehman Brothers Holdings Inc

Referring to Figure 5.4, up to January 2005 the market was moving sideways so no trading opportunities were presented. The 50-day SMA and 200-day SMA crossover occurred in October 2004.

- **A:** On Friday 13 May 2005 the first opportunity to go long occurred, marked as 'A'. What we did not know in October 2004 was if the market was going to continue moving sideways – so we wait for the market to approach the 200-day SMA, as it has at 'A'. As we eye the chart to the left we notice that this point is also close to the high reached in January 2004. We therefore expect some support here and this is also the point which the 200-day SMA is close to. Our stop is 2N, below the 200-day SMA line.

- **B:** At this point we would have been stopped out of our long position. We were kept in the trade from point A in May 2005 to 12 June 2006. What we DO NOT do is enter a short position until the market approaches the 200-day SMA again. This is so we do not get caught in a sideways market where we could be forced into a position that may not be fruitful. We address the issue of when to get into a trade by exercising some discipline and patience – timing is the key to using SMA crossover strategies.

- **C:** With an all-time high being set in February 2007, our first indication that the market may be running out of steam appeared when the price of Lehman Brothers dipped below the 200-day moving average at point 'C'. We need a reason to sell and as the 50-day and 200-day SMA lines change direction from north to south shortly after 'C', we wait for the price to approach the 200-day SMA for our entry.

- **D**: Our entry could have been at either of the points indicated by 'D'. The first is comforting and the second shows that there is some real resistance above 'D'. With our stop at 2N above the 200-day SMA we would have entered a short position in the first week of February 2008 and we were kept in all the way to the breakup and liquidation of Lehman Brothers in autumn 2008.

50 and 200 SMA for indices

In this example we will see clearly how using the SMAs together can help signal a change in long-term direction. Figure 5.5 shows the Dow Jones Index.

Figure 5.5: Dow Jones Index with 50-day and 200-day SMAs

At point 'A' it showed the beginning of a prolonged bear market. The longer-term picture like this can be used to suggest that any rally from 'A' is an opportunity to 'fade' the market. This term refers to institutions selling into a rally approaching the 200-day SMA. The stop would be placed above the 200-day SMA, usually at 2N ATR, as explained above.

Similarly at point 'B' we would feel comfortable in suggesting there may be a long-term rally ahead and any weakness in the market should be a buying opportunity.

10 EMA and 24 SMA – short-term trading

Figure 5.6 shows the ten-minute chart with the 10-period EMA and the 24-period SMA. For short-term trading it can be confusing to decide where entries should be made and stops should be placed.

We could use the technique mentioned before, using our lagging moving average as the stop line and calculating 2N below this line as our stop. Unfortunately, for shorter time frames such as the ten-minute chart we need to have a more flexible approach.

We are likely to be in and out of the market two to three times during the trading session so we need to apply a different set of rules. These are explained below, with reference to Figure 5.6.

Figure 5.6: GBP/USD, using 10 EMA and 24 SMA crossover on a ten-minute chart

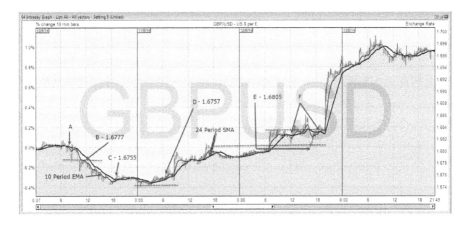

- **A**: Our first entry signal to go short – i.e. the 10-period EMA crosses the 24-period SMA. The EMA is the signal line as it crossed the SMA.

- **B**: We enter at point 'B'. The market is below the support and is touching the 10-period SMA. We do not place a stop 2N above the 24-period SMA as we did in the daily longer-term strategy described in Figures 5.1 and 5.5. Instead we seek a stop upon any break of the longer-term 24-period SMA.

- **C:** We have been stopped out of our short trade here. Our entry price at point 'B' is 1.6777 and our exit at point 'C' is 1.6755.

- **D:** There is at point 'C' another crossover of the 10-period EMA and the 24-period SMA. So we again look for some support – this time we are seeking to go long. We recognise that support exists and that the price is hugging the 10-period EMA. We go long at 'D' and have our initial stop either below the dotted support line shown or at a break of the 24-period SMA.

- **E:** Our entry price at 'D' is 1.6757. At point 'E' we note the steep decline in the 24-period SMA and note also the support indicated by the dotted line. We were stopped out here at 1.6805.

- **F:** What we notice, as time moves on, is that the crossover happens quite often after our long trade exit. It is for this reason we employ support and resistance lines to help define a good entry, whether long or short. We could have gone long at point 'F' by assuming that some longer-term support is materialising – this technique will be covered in the strategy focusing on trend lines.

9 EMA and 16 SMA for currencies – long-term trade

You may of course use a combination of EMAs and SMAs for both long and short-term charts. It is not that one is more suited to one time frame. You may find that some periods of moving averages and pairs of moving averages work better for specific asset markets, but we will not explore this topic here.

It is recommended that you open a demo account with any reputable online trading company and test some different period MAs and find the one that best suits your time frame and trading psychology.

By way of example, Figure 5.7 is the daily EUR/USD chart with the 9-day EMA and the 16-day SMA shown. Again this is a typical crossover example used by professionals.

Points to note:

- **A:** In the area marked 'A' the market was moving sideways and no real signal transpired. This is one of the disadvantages of using lagging indicators – which moving averages are. Fine-tuning using EMAs speeds up the detection process of a possible new trend. To mitigate the false signals from May to August we seek to recognise a decisive change in direction so we can be in a trade in the area marked 'B'.

- **B**: The steepness of the crossover is usually a good indicator and as soon as the 9-day EMA crossed the 16-day SMA we could have gone short with a stop above the 16-day SMA. The 16-day SMA acts as our trailing stop and should protect us against losing from a substantial rally.

Figure 5.7: EUR/USD, 9-day EMA and 16-day SMA crossover

CONCLUSION

Which moving average – simple or exponential?

Traders should experiment with different time frames. The greater the time frame the longer the lag. Lag is how long after the move in price the moving average will move. So a short time frame MA will hug the price more closely than a longer time frame MA. The ones discussed in this chapter are typical of what the professionals use.

There are differences between simple moving averages and exponential moving averages, though one is not necessarily better than the other. Exponential moving averages have less lag and are therefore more sensitive to recent prices and recent price changes. Exponential moving averages will turn before simple moving averages. Simple moving averages may be better suited to identify support or resistance levels as they include the actual data points of true prices over the given period.

Short-term moving averages (5 to 20 periods) are best suited for short-term trends and trading. Traders interested in medium-term trends would opt for longer moving averages that might extend from 20 to 60 periods. Long-term investors will prefer moving averages with 100 or more periods. This is why 200 days is important – it is not quite a year. Traders look at this to identify if a financial instrument is in a longer-term bull or bear phase, depending on if the price is actually below or above the moving average.

Disadvantages

Moving averages are trend following, or lagging, indicators that will always be a step behind. The benefit of this is that moving averages insure a trader is aware of the underlying trend and from this decisions can be made. Securities do spend a great deal of time in trading ranges, though, and this renders moving averages ineffective.

Once in a trend, moving averages will keep you in, but also give late signals. You cannot expect to sell at the top and buy at the bottom using moving averages. As with most technical analysis indicators, moving averages are best used in conjunction with other complementary tools, for instance the Relative Strength Index (RSI) or Stochastics.

Strategy 6

Trend Lines And Channels

INTRODUCTION

Our aim in this chapter is to show you how professionals apply simple trend and channel strategies in their trading. The cliché *the trend is your friend* is known to many but applied by very few.

STRATEGY BASICS

There are three ways we can trade using solely a trend and we will look at each separately with examples:

1. Trade with the trend.

2. Trade the break of a trend.

3. Trade within the channel created by the trend.

A paradox with this methodology is that many traders seek to find established trends upon which to trade from.

What if we can show you how to find a trend at its inception and also accomplish what is considered to be the most popular trading technique used by professionals (the golden entry)?

We will leave that till the end of the chapter – for now let us consider the three main trade setups listed above.

THE STRATEGY IN PRACTICE

1. Trade with the trend

The first thing to do is to draw the trend line on your chart, using the dips. This is called the line of best fit. An example is shown in Figure 6.1, a chart of Thomas Cook Group PLC (TCG).

Figure 6.1: line of best fit

Trade setup:

1. This line of best fit gives us some confidence that as the price advances it will touch this line from time to time and continue the upward trend.

2. We need to follow a basic trade management routine and ensure we have set a stop loss using a system we are comfortable with. For instance, we could use the 2N system – described in Chapter 5 – that measures the average daily movement 'N', with any movement twice this number implying a change in price direction.

3. If the price moves 2N in the direction of our trade then we should tighten our stops as volatility of this type implies a fundamental change that could impact on any profit. So we should have a method of trailing our stop loss in the direction of the trade.

Figure 6.2 shows how price touching the trend line can create trading opportunities. In this particular example, two opportunities are highlighted.

We use the 30-day Average True Range (ATR) to ensure that we are not inadvertently stopped out of a trade. In Figure 6.3 we have the example from before with two trading opportunities highlighted. The window below the price chart shows the ATR 30.

Figure 6.2: price touches the trend line and then continues the upward trend

Figure 6.3: Thomas Cook Group price chart with Average True Range 30

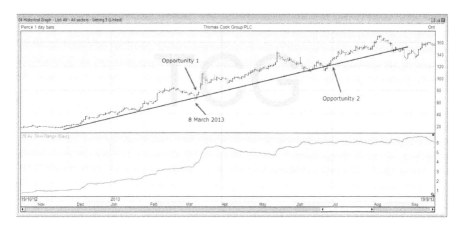

Although the price moved 6p on 8 March 2013 and the price broke below the trend line, we did not exit the trade.

ATR is just a very simple measure of volatility. It helps us monitor any increase in activity away from the average daily range that may result in a change of direction. If volatility is up then it may be enough to change the trend direction.

As we can see in Figure 6.3, ATR was around 6p on 8 March 2013, so the price movement on this day was the same as the 30-day average. When looking for a change in the trend, you are looking for a daily trading range of at least 2xATR.

2. Break of a trend

Using TCG again in Figure 6.4 we can see that applying the 2N principle and moving forward a couple of months the price broke through our preferred line of best fit. On 15 August 2013, the price moved 18p. This is 3N, as you can see the ATR is around 6p in August.

We would tighten our stops at this point. Indeed, a few days later the break below the trend occurred, exiting our long position and triggering a short position. At the time of writing we are still in the short trade as the price rose to test the line before reversing and then starting to drift sideways.

Figure 6.4: a change of trend direction in TCG

3. Trade within the channel

To trade within the channel, the first thing to do is to draw the trend line, using the **dips**, and then duplicate that line against the **peaks**, finding in both cases the **line of best fit**. This will create your channel. Once we have done this we can already draw some conclusions:

- As the price approaches the trend line connecting the dips, we look to go long, and vice versa as the price approaches the trend line connecting the peaks we look to exit our long trades and potentially enter a short position. We can continue this trading pattern for as long as the channel continues. See Figure 6.5, once again a chart for TCG. We should of course exercise our trade management rules to enter and exit our trades.

- Notice that the channel continued for eight months with potentially two opportunities to go long and three to go short, with the last short position potentially being a longer-term short position as the price moves away from the channel.

Figure 6.5: a channel in Thomas Cook Group

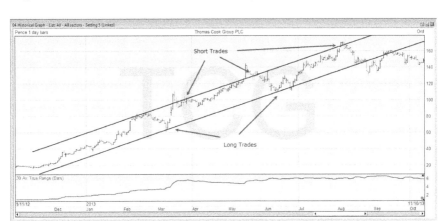

The golden entry – trend inception

We are now going to look at something we refer to as the *golden* entry. These opportunities do not occur very often. They are long-term trades and it can often take months or years for a setup to be established.

Let's look at Figure 6.6, where we have an 18-month lead up to our setup in TCG. The trend inception can often be found after sustained consolidation and here we can see that TCG moved in a sideways channel for almost 12 months after a prolonged downward movement from April 2011. You could of course have traded the range during this sideways price movement to make regular income.

This sideways range from September 2011 to October 2012 is an example of one of the most interesting setups for finding the inception of a potential new trend. Looking at no other indicators and solely at price movement and possibly volume we should poise ourselves for **any movement**, whether up or down, as we do not know which way the price may turn.

Figure 6.6: the 18 months leading up to a golden entry in TCG

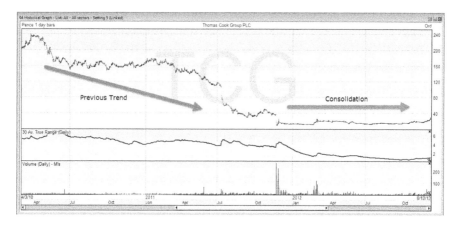

In the case of TCG we will look at what happened after October 2012, pointing out that the ATR is below 5p. We look for a breakout of the channel, increased volume and a move that is greater than 2N.

In Figure 6.7, note:

- Increased volume.

- The uptick in ATR.

- Breaking out of the consolidation area.

We enter long at the point marked on the chart.

Figure 6.7: breakout from the consolidation area

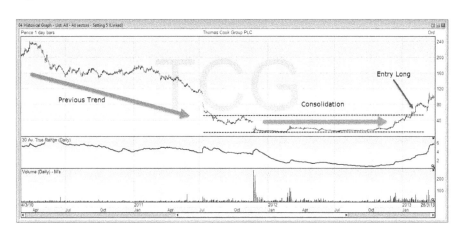

This led us to another sustained rally for the next 12 months – hence making this a longer-term trade. See Figure 6.8.

If you had not got into the trade at the point of the golden entry then further opportunities to join it are also marked on the chart.

Figure 6.8: a sustained rally away from the consolidation range

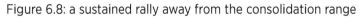

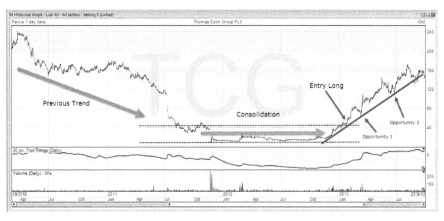

Further examples of the golden entry setup

Xaar PLC

What you will notice time and time again is that when consolidation occurs over several months, as with Xaar in Figure 6.9, the potential breakout is significant.

Figure 6.9: golden entry in Xaar PLC

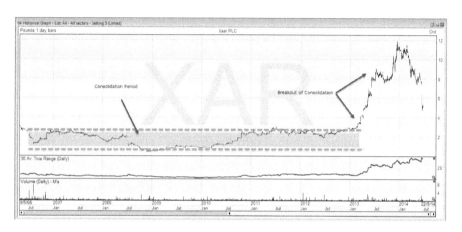

Rolls-Royce Group PLC

Two opportunities occurred with Rolls-Royce over two years. See Figure 6.10.

As with Xaar, you notice opportunities to go long where consolidation – or sideways movement – occurred for much of the year. The patient trader will always make good profits, but must not neglect to place stop losses.

Figure 6.10: two golden entry opportunities in Rolls-Royce PLC

Admiral Group

Figure 6.11 shows a chart of Admiral Group, where consolidation occurred at high levels before a break to the short side. These particularly are fortunate setups if you can spot them. Where stocks tend to take months and even years to go up, they can fall quite suddenly and the risk is usually greater, and so stops are an absolute must with short positions.

Figure 6.11: a golden short trade in Admiral Group PLC

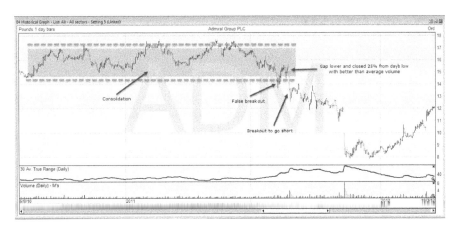

ARM Holdings

Another point to note with the golden entry is that if the consolidation period is long enough and the price range is large enough you could trade the range and go long at the bottom of the range and short at the top, as in the ARM Holdings example in Figure 6.12. Here the range trade is over 150p.

The opportunity shown here is appropriate as a channel trade and also a golden breakout trade setup.

Figure 6.12: a channel trade and golden trade setup

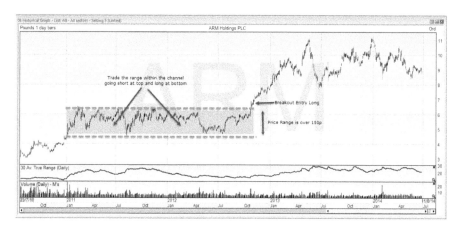

CONCLUSION

We have looked at several trend following trade setups and as you can see we could just concentrate on a single security to achieve our goal of finding all the possible opportunities. The examples from Thomas Cook Group show very clearly how shares trend up as well as down for prolonged periods and we should use common sense to enter and exit our trades.

Always remember to apply trade management and stop losses to secure profits and limit your losses.

Strategy 7

Japanese Candlesticks

INTRODUCTION

Japanese candlesticks have a long history, with over 400 years of use in the Orient. The technique is not complicated, even though it was created for use in markets that would be unfamiliar to traders today.

Rice farmers in Japan would plot the movements of rice prices using candlesticks. They discovered that particular patterns of candlesticks occurred before certain types of price moves. The patterns enabled them to discover that human psychology played an important part in the way people behave and the way prices move. This began a strong desire to make future price predictions by looking only at price movements as depicted by candlesticks.

In this chapter we will look at common candlestick patterns that precede price moves. These patterns are a depiction of human psychology. For example, the 'engulfing bear' pattern – where the price opens higher than yesterday but due to selling throughout the day closes lower than yesterday – has behind it the psychology that traders just didn't have any more buying power left and only sellers remain, so the pattern often precedes a continued down move over the next few trading periods.

It should be noted that candlesticks give you the precise sentiment of herd mentality. A single candle can depict the psychology of the market. This is a powerful tool.

It is not our intention here to give a detailed course on candlesticks – we only introduce the concept and provide you with a small number of trade setups using some simple ideas. You should seek alternative specialist knowledge on how best to trade these patterns.

Candlestick formation

At the very basic level, a candlestick can depict either an up period (a minute, day, week, month, etc.) or a down period in the market. These two forms are shown in Figure 7.1.

Usually if the market is up in the period defined by the candlestick then the real body of the candlestick will be white or green – this is called a hollow candlestick. If the market is down the real body of the candlestick will be black or red – this is called a filled candlestick.

Figure 7.1: hollow and filled candlesticks

Hollow candlestick

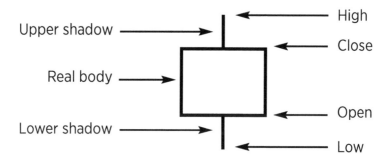

Filled candlestick

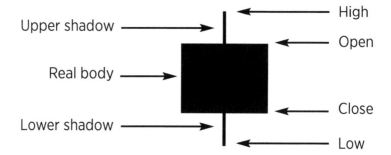

Figure 7.2 shows how a candlestick price chart looks.

Figure 7.2: a candlestick price chart showing hollow and filled candlesticks

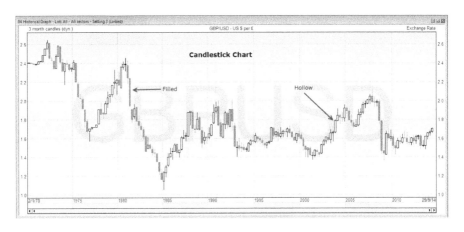

STRATEGY BASICS

A candlestick chart is a slightly more sophisticated visual representation of the bar chart.

Candlestick patterns demonstrate trader sentiment during a particular period of time – they have a psychological explanation behind them. This enables traders to develop trading strategies. Examples of different patterns are shown below, with comments on the psychology behind them. This is by no means an exhaustive list of the types of patterns – for more information you should seek a more detailed resource on candlesticks. We also give our view on how accurate the pattern tends to be for predicting price action in our experience.

Bearish shooting star

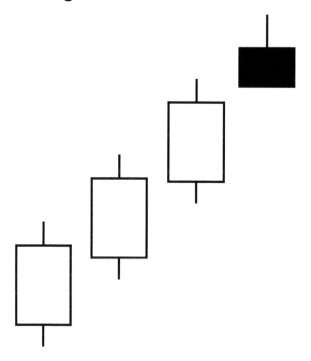

Psychology

The prices are driven higher and close higher for three consecutive days (or whatever period is in question). On the final day, prices move higher again and they even close higher than on the previous day, but the sellers drive them to close near the lower end of the range for that particular day. This suggests that buying pressure has lost momentum and a change in direction is imminent.

Accuracy

55%. This is better than a coin toss but because the final move is often small it can be as low as 55%, which is not great. We always take note of the bearish shooting star, however, because it is common and it is a popular pattern with traders.

Bearish evening doji star

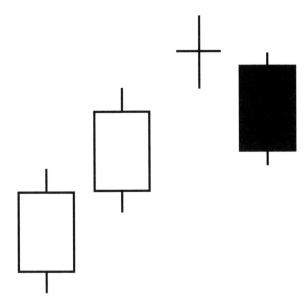

Psychology

The price rises for two days before momentum shows some weakness on the third day when the open and closing prices are the same, even though the price gapped higher from the close on the second day.

On the fourth day the price opens lower and closes lower, suggesting the bullish run is over and prices will continue to fall.

Accuracy

70%. This is our favourite pattern and one we like to take notice of. It has a high accuracy and is popular among traders.

Bearish engulfing pattern

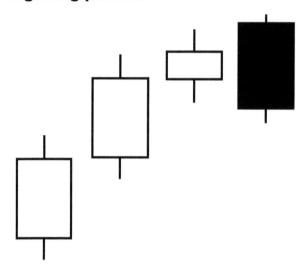

Psychology

The final day in the pattern opens higher than the previous day and closes below it. This suggests that traders tried to continue the momentum of the previous few days by forcing prices to open higher but were unable to get the buy orders and the market was so weak it even traded below the previous day's lowest point.

Accuracy

65%. This is another fairly accurate pattern. We often wait for a down move the next day to start before going short. The same applies when it's in reverse, as a bullish engulfing pattern – we wait for an up move the next day before going long. The bullish pattern is just as accurate.

Bearish inverted hammer

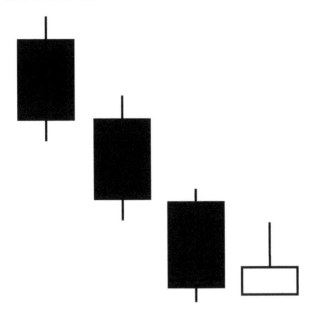

Psychology

After days of selling, the bears start to worry the falls may be coming to an end as the price tries to rise and closes up slightly compared to the previous period. The long shadow on the final day is critical. It is buyers testing the waters and this spooks bears and often marks the reversal in a downward trend.

Accuracy

55%. We always take note of this pattern because it is another popular one and the psychology behind it is strong. The accuracy is not the highest but even if the trend does not reverse at least we know it will often slow or skid sideways with ample noise. This may allow us to ease out of a short position (or a long position for the opposite pattern).

Bullish harami

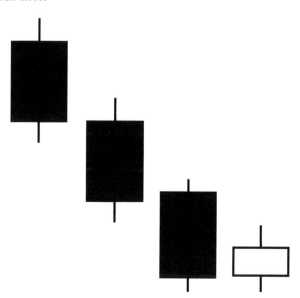

Psychology

Following a period of down days, a day occurs with a small trading range and the price closing higher than it opened. This suggests that bulls have found a floor and can fight off the selling by the bears. The buyers are able to resist falling prices.

Accuracy

55%. This follows the same principle as the bullish hammer. There is a slight difference in the psychology and the pattern as you can see, but it is very much of the same family.

This is a pattern that we trade not necessarily by going long as soon as the price moves up the next day, but on observing what the likely direction is going to be and then deciding if it makes sense to go long or if there is just too much bearish momentum and any rise may be short lived.

We make this decision by looking at other indicators, e.g. MACD, overall trend duration and direction. For instance, has the market been falling for a relatively long time and the MACD falling too sharply? If so this would suggest that the bearish movement will continue, any bullishness is a blip and we should actually sell further into any up moves as soon as the prices resumes lower.

THE STRATEGY IN PRACTICE

When looking to apply candlesticks in a straightforward way, you should look for patterns which on the close of the market will give you a reason to take a particular view and act upon this by taking a position in the market.

Below we have shown some common patterns used by professionals. Our advice is not to get too engrossed in all of the many candlestick patterns that exist. Stick to the most common and successful patterns. The patterns shown here will help you to develop a better understanding of future events in the market.

Examples of candlestick patterns

Man Group

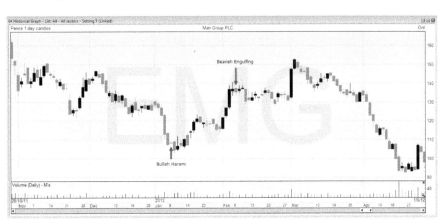

Melrose

Barclays

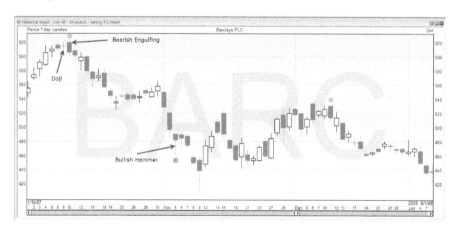

USD/JPY

Conclusion

We tend to use Japanese Candlesticks to confirm our trades. Whilst many people will use the patterns themselves, we look for additional corroborative evidence beyond the candlestick pattern – such as from one of the other strategies we have described in this book – that a move is about to happen in the direction the candlestick pattern suggests.

More Important Than Strategy

INTRODUCTION

Private traders often do not realise that more important than any trading strategy is how you use it. Professional traders will tell you that the strategy is the easy part. The difficult part is using it correctly.

In this concluding chapter we want to take you through the essential parts of all strategies that make a key difference to profit and loss. This is important because even if you have a winning strategy, if you use it incorrectly you will make a loss. Here we add the icing on the cake, to make you a winner.

3 RULES TO APPLY WHEN USING ANY STRATEGY

Rule 1: Love your small losses

Table A: gains needed to recover from losses

Drawdown (%)	Gain needed to recover (%)
5	5.3
10	11.1
15	17.6
20	25
25	33
30	42.9
40	66.7

As Table A shows, it is easy to recover from a small loss but disproportionately harder to recover from a bigger loss. If you lose 10%, you don't need a 10% gain to recover, you need an 11.1% gain – because you have 10% less money to work with.

This means you have to keep your losses small and you have to love your small losses. Professional traders have no problem with that because they know trading is not about how often you win, or how much, but how much money you preserve when you lose.

Rule 2: Know how to set stop losses

Most traders will tell you that they are unsure of where to set stop losses – a point at which you would exit the trade at a loss. Many will query if it should be a fixed percentage stop loss or a trailing stop loss. With both they discover that in volatile markets they get whipsawed – where the price falls then rebounds – and in quieter markets the price drifts down to stop them out, whereas a tighter stop closer to their entry would have saved them from such a large loss.

One of the best professional techniques therefore is the volatility-based stop. The beauty of this is it is further away in volatile markets but closer to the entry in quieter markets. It works on the basis that there is always noise in the market and when a move is beyond the noise, only then is it a signal to take notice of.

One technique we use is therefore the *average range*. The theory is that if the price moves beyond the average range then it is not noise, but a signal that something major is happening.

By average range we mean the average distance between high and low prices over a number of periods. You can look back over, say, the past 14 periods and calculate the average range per period. We then set an initial stop loss at 2x the average range on the basis that a move of twice the average range for the period indicates something may be changing in the market and we want to be out of the trade.

Most trading platforms will calculate the Average True Range (ATR) for a given time frame for you; this is pretty much the same as the average range.

Rule 3: Never lose more than 2% per trade

Whatever your stop loss, never lose more than 2% of your trading capital on a trade. This means if your initial stop loss is 2 x ATR (Average True Range) you risk 2% of your capital. If your stop is 3 x ATR then you still risk 2% of your capital.

The price chart below shows the principle in practice.

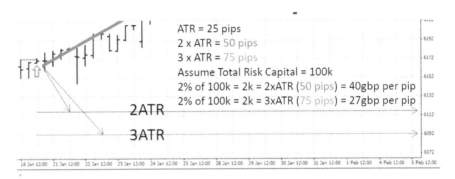

ATR = 25 pips
2 x ATR = 50 pips
3 x ATR = 75 pips
Assume Total Risk Capital = 100k
2% of 100k = 2k = 2xATR (50 pips) = 40gbp per pip
2% of 100k = 2k = 3xATR (75 pips) = 27gbp per pip

2ATR

3ATR

Note: Loss is 2% of trading capital whether price falls with a move of 2 ATR or 3 ATR.

We prefer to use 2 ATR rather than 3 ATR because with a stop loss at 3 ATR we are risking 27 GBP per pip whereas with a loss at 2 ATR we are risking 40 GBP per pip – this means with a stop loss at 2 ATR you have staked more per pip and you will thus win more per pip on winning trades; therefore your winning trades are more profitable.

Conclusion

A strategy without an understanding of how to preserve losses is no more than a fast car without an understanding of how to drive. In this chapter we wanted to emphasise that you must love your small losses and set stop losses accordingly so as to avoid the kinds of large falls which could wipe out many months of building up profits.

We wish you good luck and the discipline with which to execute your trades well.

How to Win at Spread Betting

An analysis of why some people win, some lose and
how you can be a winner

No other book has ever provided this kind of vital information - the kind that
traders need to win at spread betting. The authors have taken data from the
daily trades of hundreds of traders over a five-year period – tens of thousands
of trades. Then they analysed it. This analysis has allowed them to answer the
following questions:

- Which clients win and lose? What are their characteristics?
- Which markets are the easiest to make money on? Which markets should
retail investors avoid?
- Do investors make more money in volatile markets or quiet markets?
- Which is more profitable: to go long or to go short?
- Do short-term/day traders make more money than long-term traders?
- Which trading systems work best?
- Do technical analyst traders outperform fundamental analysis traders?
- What rules do profitable traders use for setting trade size and stop losses?
- How many spread betters win and how many lose?
- Do losers become winners and winners become losers over time?

- And much more!

What does success look like? What puts someone in the top 10 of spread
betters? What are they doing right? That is what this book teaches.

The book is packed with hardcore insider data – taken from other traders and
the authors' own trades – all carefully dissected to provide you with the
answers you need to succeed.

As insiders, the authors' aim is to show you how to beat the market. They now it
can be done because they know the winners who do it. In this book, they show
you how to do it.